WHERE IS
THE FREE LUNCH??

WHERE IS
THE FREE LUNCH??
THE VOTER'S GUIDE TO
GOVERNMENT ECONOMIC POLICY

William C. Cates

Illustrated by Bo Brown

THOMOND PRESS
An Elsevier Professional Publication

Thomond Press is an imprint of Elsevier North Holland, Inc.
52 Vanderbilt Avenue, New York, New York 10017

Distribution to the book trade in the United States
by Van Nostrand Reinhold Company.

Library of Congress Cataloging in Publication Data

Cates, William C
    Where is the free lunch??

    Bibliography: p.
    Includes index.
    1. United States—Economic policy—1971-   I. Title.
HC106.7.C38   338.973   80-14406
ISBN 0-444-00450-5

Desk Editor   Philip Schafer
Design   Edmée Froment
Design Assistant   Virginia Kudlak
Illustrator   Bo Brown and Vantage Art, Inc.
Production Manager   Joanne Jay
Compositor   Lexigraphics
Printer   Haddon Craftsmen

Manufactured in the United States of America

To Barbara and all others
who only audited Economics 101

CONTENTS

PREFACE

The origin of this book is my experience on the international side of the United States Treasury Department between 1970 and 1973, a period which included one of the major upheavals of this century: the United States departure from the Gold Exchange Standard. Looking back on that experience it dawned on me that neither I nor, to the best of my knowledge, anybody around me was aware of what was really happening to us. The scene resembled a Krazy Kat cartoon with the cats intently analysing one hole in the baseboard, while the mice trooped out through another. Government officials were agonizing over the American balance of payments that was threatened by Japanese, Canadians, and Europeans, all selling their goods here at cheap prices because they pegged their currencies to the dollar at artificially low rates. Elaborate studies about the price elasticities of demand for imports and exports at different exchange rates streamed across each government desk. (None of them will appear in these pages.)

While we all contemplated this mousehole, the Federal Reserve Board, a few blocks up Constitution Avenue, was allowing the world to be flooded with surplus dollars created by the American and European banking systems. It was here that the mischief lay.

As the drama unfolded, we at the Treasury Department were treated to long instructive seminars in which many of the nation's most prominent economists participated. If they knew what was happening, they didn't get it across—at least not to me.

During these years I had a colleague, who became a rare Washington friend, Dr. Wilson Schmidt, on leave from the chairmanship of the Department of Economics of Virginia Politechnic Institute. We regularly discussed economic questions of every nature. Whenever I ran across a new idea and bounced it off Wilson, his reaction was instant and incisive: "Is it in the literature?" The "literature" is that body of academic journals through which economists communicate with one another in sine and cosine language. From Wilson I gathered that if an idea was in the "literature," it was already full-fledged and ready for a computer; if not, it didn't exist.

The author intends no unkindness or disrespect towards economists. Unkindness and disrespect to any group of people constitutes discrimination, which is un-American and, in public places, illegal.

However, the book is dedicated to the idea that economics, and particularly government economic policy, has become too important a part of our lives to be left exclusively to economists. There is probably no idea in this book that is not in the "literature" *somewhere,* at least mirrored in an exposition of the opposite. But the "literature" of economics, in common with that of most academic disciplines, exists for its own economic reason: to provide university administrations with grounds for granting tenure and promotion. Its content is buried. My purpose is to bring some ideas out from under the "literature" and into the light.

The lay reader may ask, why is this for me? The same question might have been asked about sex education (had it been offered) in the Victorian Age. Why not just lie down and accept? The economic priesthood today would probably agree with that point of view, just as the clerical priesthood encouraged an attitude of demure ignorance in the last century. In economics as in sex education there is a middle ground between the Harlequin Romance style of a Paul Erdman and the Masters and Johnson approach of a Paul Samuelson. I am looking for that middle ground and for the reader who enjoys the whimsy of things that are taken very seriously elsewhere. In particular I hope that people of student age will read this before deciding whether or not to major in economics.

ACKNOWLEDGMENTS

I would like to express my gratitude to a number of specialists who took the trouble to read and comment on early drafts of selected chapters. They include W.H. Bruce Brittain, Michael W. Keran, David P. Stuhr, Paul A. Volcker, Ralph A. Young. None of them have seen the final manuscript and they are, of course, in no way responsible for content or opinion.

As to style and clarity, if this book is at all readable, that is due in large measure to the patient efforts of my wife, Inge, foreign-born and a noneconomist, who did the final editing and would not clear a single sentence that she herself did not find fully comprehensible.

I am indebted to Nursat Aygen for valuable research assistance and to Helen Ring for typing the manuscript.

William H. Mogan of Elsevier North Holland provided, from start to finish, the kind of guidance and encouragement that keeps an author going.

WHERE IS
THE FREE LUNCH??

1

THE "DISMAL SCIENCE"

All economic movements, by their very nature, are motivated by crowd psychology.

BERNARD BARUCH, 1932

Shortly after being thrust into office, President Gerald Ford took the unprecedented step of convening the cream of America's economists to a public meeting at the White House. The agenda: how best to steer the ship of state between the Scylla of inflation and the Charybdis of recession. The twenty eight professors assembled covered the spectrum of "respectable" economics; from John Kenneth Galbraith, articulate critic of capitalist society, to Milton Friedman, staunch defender of *laissez-faire*. The proceedings were broadcast for an entire day on public television.

Economists are not famous for their ability to agree about anything, but on this occasion the consensus was remarkable. The vast majority advocated vigorous steps to combat the menace of the moment: inflation. That was early in September 1974. By December of the same year it was glaringly apparent that America and the world were plunging into their worst depression in 40 years. A bewildered President was obliged to shift gears fast, and he must have wondered to himself how so much impressive talent could have misled him so thoroughly.

That televised September conclave probably marked the high point of public reverence for economists. After such a forecasting fiasco, not only has the public begun to doubt economists, economists have begun to doubt themselves. Meanwhile, college students are turned off in droves by introductory economics courses that seem to offer little clue to reality.

Economics has often been called the "dismal science." The contention of this book is that it is neither dismal nor a science, because economics is the study of people and how they behave when their pocketbooks are at stake. The behavior of people is the stuff of comedy and sometimes tragedy, but people rarely act according to laws of scientific predictability.

One possible way to define an "economy" is a group of individuals whose collective effort produces a measurable result. Such a definition puts the focus on the interaction between resources available and the intelligence, drive, and morale of the people exploiting them. An economy can be of any size—a family farm, a nation, or the whole world—provided its population and output can be identified and measured.

At any given instant the resources available to a population are finite. People have to make do with what they have. Over time, however, resources can be expanded by human frugality and ingenuity, provided there is an incentive to save and to invent. An example that immediately springs to mind is the vast difference in productivity between large collective farms and small private plots in the Soviet Union. Despite overwhelming government allocation of land and labor to the former, it is estimated by Soviet sources that 27% of the total agricultural output comes from the one percent of land left in private hands.[1] It is in private farming for private gain that the incentive for ingenuity and frugality resides.

A major reason why economics has achieved a reputation for dullness, and recently for inadequacy as well, is that most economists are loath to recognize the very large human element—crowd psychology—that is inherent in the functioning of any economy. In pursuit of science, they understandably prefer to confine their work to statistically measurable variables, stirring as many as possible of them into a computer to produce numerical results, precise to the last decimal.

These results are likely to be as misleading as they are precise, for the human factor—the most important and challenging ingredient—is left out. Why people behave the way they do;

Economists take a scientific approach

what causes alternate moods of euphoria and despair, booms and busts, is one of the most fascinating unexplored areas of knowledge.

Because human behavior is what makes an economy tick, the ability to influence this behavior is the touchstone of government economic policy. Russia and China have relied upon exhortation, peer criticism and the police, with less than inspiring results. The American Government has at times also resorted to exhortation—from Roosevelt's clarion "Nothing to fear but fear itself" to Carter's limp "Moral equivalent of war"—but these efforts have also been without conspicuous success. Unfortunately, the hows and whys of collective human behavior, because they are poorly understood, are largely ignored. As a result, government efforts to do something about the economy have rarely been successful and frequently been disastrous.

It is no secret that the role of government in every national economy has burgeoned, with no end in sight. From simply keeping the peace and collecting taxes while otherwise leaving citizens to do their own thing, governments have taken on the tasks of redistributing income, supplementing individual savings with Social Security, protecting the environment, protecting workers and consumers, combating unemployment, and, most difficult of all, controlling the business cycle.

If there is a common thread running through all of these functions laid upon, or arrogated by, governments, it is the allocation of society's resources. In a completely socialist country, such as Soviet Russia, the job is theoretically simple. Endowed with absolute power, an all-wise bureaucracy can determine how much of the savings will go into armaments, industry, or agriculture. It can determine which consumer goods will be made available and in what quantities. A large part of the intellectual appeal of Marxism arises from the fact (or illusion) that socialist planners are not obliged to contend with the unpredictable passions of the population. The moral appeal lies in the presumption that bureaucrats deciding the fate of others are more disinterested and therefore more virtuous than ordinary mortals pursuing the padding of their own pocketbooks.

Governments of capitalist countries cannot directly determine the allocation of resources. When they try, the result is apt to be long lines at the gasoline pump. They must play the subtler game of influencing the collective behavior of their populations. To exert this influence they have limited arsenals of carrots and sticks. The carrots are principally tax incentives— otherwise called "loopholes." If the nation needs more oil or needs to conserve its use, government can offer the carrot of a tax incentive to anyone who drills for oil or who insulates his house. The sticks lie in the regulatory woodshed. Government can exact penalties for pollution of the environment, inadequate attention to worker safety, harmful consumer products, false advertising, concentration of business power, and a myriad of other offenses, great and small, that the self-interested individual constantly seems to be perpetrating upon the rest of society.

These sticks and carrots can nudge the nation a little bit in one direction or another, but the greater drama that captures economists' and the public's attention is how fast the economy is going, not whither. Stimulation of the economy and avoidance of recessions have been the conspicuous challenges for all Western governments since the Great Depression of the 1930's. These challenges were fairly well met during the 1950's and 1960's, at least in the sense that most Western governments were unable to get in the way of basic economic forces propelling the world to ever higher levels of output and consumption.

For the past decade, however, government growth policies have been notoriously unsuccessful in most nations, including the United States. Budget deficits and money creation, called, respectively, fiscal policy and monetary policy, have combined to give us "stagflation" and what President Carter calls a national *"malaise."* How and why this has happened will be discussed later. At this point, it is sufficient to note that every government policy has its psychological side effects. When government makes a major move, it does not just drop a big statistic into the economic mechanism. It flashes a signal to the hopes and fears of living, breathing people. Popular response to that signal will determine the success or failure of the policy.

The signals emanating from both fiscal and monetary policies in recent years have spelled inflation. Together with signals from other government policies, particularly in regulation and energy, they have also spelled uncertainty. Altogether, these signals and the reality of rising taxation have helped to cause a dangerous slowdown in the pace of investment and innovation, both of which are necessary for the nation's growth. Consumers, fearing the ravages of inflation, rush to buy anything tangible: real estate, art, jewelry, gold.

The signals of inflation and uncertainty emanating from Washington have a particularly perverse effect on investors, the people who must make decisions about the use of their personal savings or the savings—corporate and pension fund— entrusted to their management. These individual decisions, made by or on behalf of savers, determine both the pace and the allocation of national investment. They therefore determine the rate and direction of national growth. A Congress or an administration that genuinely wishes to stimulate the economy, reduce unemployment, or pursue particular policy objectives, such as the development of domestic sources of energy, *must recognize this fact.* The only alternative to recognition of the role of private investment is nationalization of several or all sectors of American industry so that thereafter investment can be allocated by a selfless—and faceless—bureaucracy. With a few exceptions, such as Amtrak, TVA, and certain recent energy proposals, this alternative has been firmly rejected by the American people.

The myriad of investment decisions that determine the course of the American economy are taken in corporate board rooms and at banks across the country and in the "financial community" centered on Wall Street. Every investment decision is a gamble—though the odds are real rather than artificial—taken in the hope of gain and the fear of loss, and always in the presence of uncertainty. When government adds to this uncertainty, it delays and inhibits investment. When it promises to penalize any investment success with a capital gains tax or a windfall profits tax, it shuts off the investment altogether. People can be scared into buying gold, but they cannot be scared into building plants and machinery.

The hub and barometer of the American economy—the closest thing to a central planning board—is the stock market. Although the actual decisions on whether to build a plant, where to locate it, and what it should produce are made far from Wall Street, the stock market is not far from the minds of the decision-makers. For, the "bottom line" for corporate executives is not just earnings, it is how stockholders, present and potential, will look at these earnings, and whether they will expect the earnings to increase in the future. In short, the bottom line is the price of the stock, in which, by the way, most executives have options that either will be a nice nest egg or will be worthless.

High stock prices, for the market as a whole as well as for individual industries and companies, have a dual effect on investment. When the price of its stock is high, it is easy for a company to sell stock to the public and thereby get new equity financing for expansion. This is particularly important for smaller companies that often pioneer new directions for the economy to take. There is also the purely psychological effect. A high stock price produces a glow in the corporate boardroom and makes the risk of building a new plant loom less large.

Low stock prices obviously have the opposite effect: rather than building new plants, it often makes more sense for a company to buy in its own stock at bargain prices or to try to take over the assets of another company whose stock is even cheaper. The story of the 1970's has been low stock prices, low investment, and unprecedented rates of stock repurchase and corporate takeovers. Even the Joint Economic Committee of Congress has taken note of the possible cause and effect relationship between low stock prices and a low rate of investment.[2]

The purpose of dwelling on the role of the stock market in determining the rate and direction of economic development is to emphasize, once again, the element of mob psychology. The stock market is a very psychological place. As such, it is anathema to most economists. The textbook explanation of resource allocation usually goes as follows: "What things will be produced is determined by the dollar votes of consumers. . . ."[3] This explanation makes no mention of the dollar votes of *investors* and leaves out all the uncertainties that surround any forecast of what "the dollar votes of consumers" *will be* once a plant has been built and is in operation for five to ten years. Professor Paul A. Samuelson, Nobel Laureate and the nation's top economic textbook writer, is fond of saying that the stock market has predicted nine of the past five recessions. A better way of putting it, however, might be that four of the last nine stock market slumps failed, miraculously, to spill over onto the economy as a whole.

Samuelson also takes the viewpoint of a true intellectual when he writes, "The best brains in Wall Street scarcely do as well as the averages."[4] The statement is quite true, though it leaves one wondering whether or not the few successes of some better-than-the-best brains managed to provoke academic jealousy. The question is not: Are investors as a group wiser or more foolish than professors? Rather, it is: Do the collective judgments that are reflected in stock prices have an influence on the pace and direction of economic activity? Is the stock market a barometer that makes the weather?

If this thought might be disturbing to economists, it is positively repugnant to politicians. In America, the stereotype of an investor in the stock market is that of a "Fat Cat" skinning the hide of the "Common Man." This was perhaps the case up until 1929, but by now the stock market is less colorful. The big rollers on Wall Street today are typically rather insecure individuals who have been hired to manage pension funds, mutual funds, and the trust departments of banks, all of them investing the savings of the Common Man himself.

These "institutional portfolio managers" as a group are fully as volatile, if not so venal, as the speculators of the 1920's. What they have to lose is their jobs, and quite possibly the chance of finding any other job in the same field. They are as fearful of failing to make money in a rising market as they are of losing money in a falling one. If they do not "do as well as the averages," they are in trouble. In a bull market they are the heroes of best-selling nonfiction;[5] in a bear market they move furtively, hoping not to get caught with the wrong stock or without the right one. They are the perfect material for sudden mass movements in any direction. And, where they move, if the movement is sustained, the economy is likely to follow.

But, it is the stereotype rather than the reality that determines political attitudes toward investment. If investors lose money, it is politically acceptable; if they make money, it is sinful. Given such moral bookkeeping, it becomes difficult to sustain a healthy rate of investment. Only in the past year or two has it been possible for public figures to speak openly about the crying need for new investment to restore productivity and growth in this country. But, to acknowledge the need for a healthy stock market before any such investment can be undertaken would still require an act of extreme political courage. Allen Greenspan, then Chairman of President Ford's Council of Economic Advisors, remarked on television during the 1975 recession that the worst sufferers had been stockbrokers. The embarrassment to the Ford Administration was acute. Nevertheless, the stock market is a crowd upon whose psychology an intelligent government can play to further the national interest. To play on it requires only the tacit admission that those who take investment risks must be allowed to reap commensurate rewards.

It is at this point that economic questions become questions of ethics and social values. One of these questions is, should everybody's income be as equal as possible, or should people be given every opportunity to advance in a society that is inherently unequal? Many Western countries, led by Britain and Sweden, have been moving towards ever greater income redistribution through confiscatory tax rates. This has the unintended effect of freezing social classes. Those who have already made or inherited their wealth are rendered secure from the rivalry of upstart *nouveaux riches,* because under today's income taxes it is nearly impossible for the aspiring to acquire substantial wealth. Many intellectuals also find high income taxes convenient and therefore moral: their patrons can be found among families with second or third generation wealth, and their prestige does not require a large after-tax income. From such heights it is easy to express "becoming concern" for the poor.

The question remains, which is the fairer society and which is the more dynamic society: one in which new faces can rise to the top or one in which incomes are leveled and status frozen?

Another question arises to plague seekers after utopia. Is unequal distribution of income and wealth less "democratic" than unequal distribution of power and prestige? For, in a perfectly egalitarian society the able and ambitious will train their talents almost exclusively towards acquisition of direct power over their fellow men and women. A brief sojourn in either Moscow or Washington, D.C., will drive this point home even to the most naive. Whatever the apparent differences between these two capitals, in neither city is the name of the game dollars or rubles. It is power and perquisites.

These and many other philosophical questions will arise in any discussion of government economic policy. They have no clear-cut answers, but they deserve to be faced squarely and honestly. Economics is not a numbers game. It involves an appreciation of human motivation and a constant questioning of ethical beliefs, one's own and those of society as a whole.

If there is a "free lunch" to be had in economics, it should be named for the last of the Spirits to emerge from Pandora's box: hope. Once people have the hope that their efforts and their ingenuity will bring about a better life for them or for their children, they will be as happy as humans are capable of being. The economy will be vibrant.

When the hope for advancement—material or spiritual—disappears, consumption cannot fill the void. Then even freedom loses its meaning, for it is hope that animates freedom.

2

THE REAL WORLD

We should always remember a slight tendency on the part of
people in my profession to say that recessions are acts of God, and
the recovery is brought about by economists.

JOHN KENNETH GALBRAITH
Meet the Press, July 9, 1978

Ingenuity, hard work, and frugality on the family farm will be
of little avail in the face of a prolonged drought. Similarly, the
best of government policies cannot protect nations against sudden adverse changes in the resources available to them. Nor,
can bad government completely block the tide of progress
when that tide is running.

Government did not invent the steam engine. No amount of
central planning could have produced the telephone. Not even
price controls, no matter how strict, can yield the cost savings of
the cotton gin or the computer. Neither a budget deficit nor
easy money can endow a nation with fertile plains and an indus-
trious population. These truisms are a reminder that there is a
real world outside the air-conditioned offices of bureaucrats, a
world in which forces contend and events occur that frequently
make government policy irrelevant. These forces and events,
usually quite unpredictable, have a far greater impact upon our
jobs and our prosperity than any measures a government—
capitalist or socialist—can possibly take. If the harvest of the
real world is plentiful, governments will try to take the credit. If
the real world produces trouble, the politicians in office are
given the blame and usually the boot.

What has been going on in that real world beyond the New Frontier, the Great Society, and the populist pulpit?

The unprecedented growth and prosperity enjoyed by the West after World War II—a success story that ended abruptly in the early 1970's—was widely touted as the product of official cleverness. Economic policy-makers believed they had discovered the philosophers' stone, which they sometimes called "fine tuning," whereby good government guaranteed higher and higher incomes for everybody each and every year of their lives. In fact, the leaders of Japan and the Western World were riding a wave not of their own making. Postwar prosperity was rooted in four unique phenomena, each of which was bound to run its course. Alas, all came to an end at about the same time.

The first phenomenon of postwar prosperity was recovery from the war itself. Western Europe and Japan had hit bottom and, as if on a trampoline, had nowhere to go but up. American foreign aid, without historical precedent for generosity and intelligence, kindled sparks on the ready tinder of local initiative. Devastation was the opportunity for renovation, and for the best part of 25 years Europe and Japan bounced giddily upward, with America the inspiration and model for their recovery. Trade grew apace, reflecting the growing prosperity of the Old World back upon the New.

However, like the upward thrust of a trampoline, the momentum of any recovery has its limits. Both Europe and Japan reached them probably in the early Seventies.

The second engine of postwar growth was a near revolution in agricultural technique. According to one expert, from the beginnings of agriculture until 1950 most of the year-to-year increases in world food output came from expansion of the area under cultivation. But since 1950 some four-fifths of the gains in output came from more intensive cultivation on existing land area.[1] Unfortunately, fertilizers, pesticides, and even hybrid seeds also have their limits. The spectacular growth of world food production, which had kept world food prices on an even keel for two decades despite rapidly rising populations, came to an abrupt end in 1972. Due in part to crop failures in the Soviet Union that year, the world price of wheat tripled between 1972 and the end of 1973.[2] Overall food prices in

America rose 43% in 1973 alone. Another prop to prosperity had disappeared.

At about the same time, a different food source peaked out: from 1950 to 1970 fish had furnished an ever-increasing part of the human diet, but in 1970 this trend was abruptly reversed. Since 1970 there has been an 11% decline in the per capita fish catch throughout the world.[3]

The third underpinning of the Western and Japanese economic miracles was cheap energy. For twenty-five years, the cost of Middle East oil fell, even as the demand for it soared. The abundance of this oil lent wings to the growth of the industrialized world, whose peoples and governments remained oblivious to the sand upon which their castles were built. Awareness came with an embargo in 1973 followed by a fourfold price increase.

Finally, in the early Seventies we woke up to ecology, and realized that postwar prosperity had been founded upon a fourth, shameful, cornerstone: the abuse of the world we inhabit. Repairing the damage already done is and will continue to be costly. Ensuring against further damage will inevitably inhibit future growth.

Thus, in the first half of the 1970's four of the major forces that had been propelling world growth for a quarter century either stopped pushing or reversed direction. A generation of Westerners and Japanese, accustomed to steady yearly increases in their living standards, suddenly found themselves going nowhere or even falling backwards.

These very real troubles have inevitably caused psychological trauma in intellectual circles. "Growth is Dead" has become the theme song of voluminous tracts about the world economy. The first and most famous of these was *The Limits of Growth*, published in 1972 by the Club of Rome, a prestigious group of industrialists, scientists, economists, and sociologists, which warned that we had about reached the limits of our planet's capacity to support people and industry. The scarcity theme has been taken up by many others.

While frequently impressive, these arguments should be taken with a grain of salt. For one thing, they are scarcely new. Malthus made precisely the same prophecies 180 years ago:

population would outstrip resources. For another, the "no growth" syndrome is an understandable outgrowth of the sudden change in fortune to which the people of the West have been subjected. During drought years morale on the family farm is apt to get a little low.

As Malthus did in his day, the doomsayers of our time overlook the potential impact of new technology—a sterile word for human innovation. This lapse is understandable, for we, like Malthus, have no way of knowing what forms—if any—this innovation will take.

One persuasively pessimistic argument revolves around the enormous and unique impact of the automobile upon economic growth. Its manufacture, together with construction of the roads and filling stations that serve it, has provided employment for millions. It has also led to a revolution in life-style, including the conquest of a new frontier, suburbia, with its Levittowns, shopping centers, and fast food restaurants.[4] Is it conceivable that the automobile revolution will be duplicated in some other form? The only answer to this question is another one: Was the automobile revolution itself conceivable?

Other innovations, from television to jet travel, have transformed lives in this postwar period while at the same time providing impetus to the most formidable growth rate in the history of mankind. What will come along to take their place, and when?

The most significant argument of the neo-Malthusian pessimists is also the most dubious. One of the key factors, they say, in the postwar economic "rocket ride" was a "public attitude that supported growth."[5] This attitude has presumably changed and, indeed, some argue that people should now be conditioned to expect lower growth rates from here on out. However, it is as likely, or more likely, that public support is the consequence, not the cause of growth.

After a look into the crystal ball of our economic future, about all one can safely conclude is that if "growth" means continued increases in output along established and predictable lines, then not only will it slow, it might well stall. If, however, growth means change, than we are bound to have it, though in directions and in a time frame that no one can foresee.

Here is where government actions can and do have their

impact on the real world. From 1948 to 1969, the American growth rate averaged 3.8% per annum, 65% higher than the annual growth rate from 1929 to 1941. According to an exhaustive study done at the Brookings Institution, this increase in our growth rate was due to "advances in knowledge" and "capital" (investment).[6] Both can be stimulated—or retarded—by government policy.

The source of "advances in knowledge" is, obviously, research and development. Spending for research and development in this country peaked in 1968 at $31 billion and by 1977 amounted to only $28 billion. As a percentage of Gross National Product, it fell from three percent to two percent. The decline in research and development spending has probably been greater than the absolute figures indicate, for much of the "research and development" expenditure of the 1970's has of necessity been devoted to satisfying the requirements of government regulators. The costs of surmounting government regulation in order to bring a new product to the market have skyrocketed (see Chapter 11), and these costs are in large part classified as research and development.

The other ingredient in our postwar growth cited by the Brookings study was capital investment. This too has slowed during the decade of the Seventies, so much so as to cause concern even in Congress. The Joint Economic Committee of House and Senate complained in its 1979 Economic Report of America's "dismal productivity performance" due to insufficient capital formation and urged "further (sic) steps to strengthen investment." (With the exception of the Investment Tax Credit passed fifteen years earlier, Congress has not been seen taking steps to encourage private investment.)

As one reason for the sluggish pace of investment, the Committee Report cited increased taxes paid by corporations as a consequence of inflation, a matter that will be discussed in detail in Chapter 9. Another major reason given in the Report already has been alluded to in Chapter 1: in the Committee's words, "The combination of high interest rates and low stock prices creates an environment that is exceedingly inhospitable to capital spending. High interest rates make borrowing costly, and low stock prices make the flotation of new capital issues difficult and unrewarding."[7]

What the lawmakers left out when listing reasons for low rates of investment during the 1970's is uncertainty over government policy itself, an uncertainty due in large part to Congressional indecision. Uncertainty is, of course, a normal fact of life. None of us can be sure what the future will bring, and all of us, including entrepreneurs, take uncertainty—otherwise called "market risk"—in our stride, win or lose. But, if an all-powerful government is in the picture with the right to tell you after you have built a house that you put it in the wrong place or that you should have used stone instead of wood, or that you can only live in it six months out of a year, you probably will not build the house in the first place. As such, the uncertainties now facing would-be corporate investors are: Will it be decreed that a new plant, once built, is in the environmentally wrong place, or that it must use coal instead of oil, or oil instead of coal, or that you are making too much money from it?

Though there are no available statistics to prove it, the likelihood is that this type of uncertainty about future government actions (and court litigation) has been a major if not the predominant reason behind the low levels of investment in America during the last decade. Laws, however draconian, can be endured. It is the economic equivalent of the midnight knock on the door that demoralizes.

To summarize, the 1970's have seen the world suddenly deprived of three strong forces for growth and prosperity: cheap energy, rapidly increasing world food production, and the momentum of postwar recovery. They also ushered in an awakening to the perils of environmental damage and the costs of its repair. These have been changes in our "real world" over which the best of government policies would have had little control. It is small wonder, then, that the United States and most other nations as well have had to take their economic lumps. Nor is it surprisng that Americans and many Europeans have become disappointed and bewildered, losing their confidence in the possibilities of growth, which is to say, in their own ingenuity.

We are still in a period of painful adjustment, and unfortunately most of the policies of Congress and the Administrations during the decade have not been helping. The process of innovation and investment that alone can enable us to start off again in new (and as yet unknown) directions has been slowed by taxes and regulatory policies to the point where there is widespread doubt about America's ability to regain its former position of economic and technological leadership.

Instead of concentrating on the development of incentives that would mobilize the nation's ingenuity and talent for the solution of real problems, our government has continued to apply time-tested remedies of the 1950's and 1960's: fiscal and monetary stimulus. These policies did relatively little harm to an economy whose progress was too powerful to be arrested by government intervention, but they are inappropriate for restoring momentum to an economy that is stalled.

Before discussing them, it is necessary to take a critical look at the statistics upon which they are founded—a vast array of numbers that constitute the grist for policy mills and the source of daily headlines in newspaper financial sections.

3

THE NUMBERS GAME

There are lies, damn lies and statistics.

MARK TWAIN

Economic policy and planning rely upon prediction. Are we headed towards inflation or recession? Or both? Are our resources, or some part of them, running out? Whence cometh the next impetus to growth? Answers to such questions must be found before policy can be made, but the record on our ability to predict the future is scarcely encouraging.

At the end of World War II, the universal expectation was for a depression that never materialized. The next major turning point, the inflation of 1973, was unforeseen by most economic forecasters, as was the severe worldwide recession that followed. It is almost axiomatic that a consensus forecast, which is the only forecast that guides governments, will never detect a major change in the offing.

The reason why such a forecast will not predict major changes is that radical predictions require shrewd analysis and the personal courage to go out on a limb. Loners are capable of this, but the consensus crowd is apt to play it safe.

This fallibility of economic forecasting has not deterred the creation of an enormous and lucrative forecasting industry. Major corporations and most brokerage firms have at least one house economist. The large banks have dozens of them. In addition, there are the econometric models of the University of Pennsylvania's Wharton School, MIT, Data Resources, Inc.,

Chase Econometrics, and others, whose impressively comput-
erized forecasts bedazzle thousands of well-paying subscribers.

However, the most that these forecasts can offer, usually, is
an estimate as to whether the current trend will be a little more
up or down. Major changes are hard to see and harder to sell.
To be commercially valid a forecast must cluster with the pack,
showing just enough originality to justify the price of the service but not so much as to risk credibility.

Such minutiae are hardly the stuff of high drama, and economic forecasters might have been relegated to producing
yawns in corporate boardrooms had it not been for the press.
The dynamics of journalism have created a tightrope psychology. In their search for a headline, financial writers regularly
depict the American economy as about to plunge into the abyss
of depression or be swept away by the winds of inflation. A half
percent change, up or down, in almost any index may cause a
fatal loss of balance. Trivia have been made newsworthy, as
have the forecasters who produce them. What does this do for
the economy itself?

Put a healthy, normal person in a hospital intensive care unit.
Wire him to every measuring device known to medical elec-
tronics and force him to look at all the squiggles displayed on
cathode tubes. If he does not die of fright first, he will readily
believe that the doctors have saved his life. In sickness and in
health the American economy is constantly monitored, with
every symptom promptly displayed to the public. To that injury
is added the institutionalized feedback of the Consumer Confidence Survey. In the morning we learn of the latest dire possi-
bility of falling off the tightrope; during the day a sample of
sensitized citizenry is polled, and at breakfast the following
morning we can read about the latest collapse of consumer
confidence.

As raw material for these Perils of Pauline there is an immense amount of numerical data. More than any other people,
with the possible exception of the Japanese, Americans worship
numbers. The major variables of our economic fever chart are
Gross National Product, Prices, Unemployment, and the
Money Supply. The Balance of International Payments used to
be included in the list, but early in the 1970's, when this was
particularly adverse, the Treasury Department concluded that
no one measurement of this balance had any real meaning.

The American economy is constantly monitored

Perhaps the same will someday be said about some of the other numbers upon which we rely.

Behind these major variables lies an infinite variety of other statistics and indices. The data available are limited only by the ability of human imagination to conjure them: farm income, housing starts, inventory accumulation or liquidation, paper board output, . . . all the way to job openings for statisticians. Combinations and permutations of these statistics offer a geometric expansion of the already infinite. One can construct indices of indices. Of these, one of the favorites is the "index of leading indicators," an essential entrail for the ritual of economic augury.

GROSS NATIONAL PRODUCT

The granddaddy of all the numbers is Gross National Product or GNP. Representing the dollar value of the nation's total output, its upward march is proof of progress. This march is helped along by, among other things, war, waste, and natural catastrophes such as earthquakes, floods, and hurricanes, which provide a lift to economic activity by requiring reconstruction. As a broad indicator, GNP tells us at least how fast we're going, if not whither.

CONSUMER PRICES

The Consumer Price Index, also called the Cost of Living Index, pervades the lives of all of us. A measure of inflation, it is in turn used to produce more inflation. Wage agreements increasingly allow for "cost of living" increases, as determined, naturally, by the Consumer Price Index. The minimum wage is periodically hiked, and Social Security payments revised, to reflect its upward lurches. Yet, this yardstick has been called, with much justification, a "statistical monstrosity."[1] Included in it are property taxes, sales taxes, and Social Security taxes. Excluded is the income tax. This logical inconsistancy is likely to tempt politicians to lower Social Security taxes rather than income taxes, because the first lowers the "cost of living" (statistically) while the second is not measured.

To construct this vital index, the Labor Department assembles a hypothetical "market basket" of goods in the proportions in which it believes the typical American family buys them. This "basket" is revised every few years to reflect changes in consumer purchasing habits. Even if these revisions were timely, which they are not, they cannot allow for everyday substitution as prices change (pork for beef, chicken for hamburger, TV Guide for Playboy). We would all have to be preprogrammed robots to shop the way the Labor Department says we shop and to pay what the Consumer Price Index says we pay.

UNEMPLOYMENT

Compared with the published unemployment rate, the Consumer Price Index is a model of conceptual logic and measurement accuracy. After all, "statistical monstrosity" is tame compared with "an abomination, an Alice-in-Wonderland stew of apples, oranges, and red herrings," the words chosen by Professor Peter F. Drucker to describe unemployment statistics.[2]

We normally think of someone unemployed as having lost his or her job because of a recession and desperately looking for another job to feed the family. Or we think of an underprivileged youth unable to find a job at the local grocery store or filling station. However, a study done at the National Bureau of Economic Research, one of the oldest and most prestigious economic research institutions in the country, found that less than half of those counted as unemployed were actually looking for work.

Lumped into the number of unemployed, or the "unemployment rate" that hits the newspaper headlines each month are, not only truly unemployed full-time breadwinners, but also the following: those who are seeking temporary work, those who are on temporary layoff and collecting unemployment insurance, those who are looking for jobs but are not yet available for work, and those who are in-between jobs which, by their very nature, are temporary, including construction work and substitute teaching.[3]

Adding to this conceptual confusion is an artificial increase in the unemployment figures due to a "conservative" measure passed by Congress under the Nixon Administration. As of July 1, 1972, persons wishing to qualify for food stamps and Aid to Families with Dependent Children were required to register for work. According to one study these registration requirements alone added nearly two percentage points to overall unemployment on average during the period from 1974 to mid-1978.[4]

The measurement of unemployment is based on raw material from a monthly survey of households conducted by the Census Bureau. An adult member of each household is asked questions about every member of the household. As the National Bureau study gently puts it, "the central problem of measuring unemployment is to convert the answers to a long series of questions into a judgment whether a person is unemployed, employed, or out of the work force." One of the survey questions asks, "What has X been doing in the last four weeks to find work?" Although the interviewer is not supposed to ask leading questions, the questionnaire itself contains the following possible answers: "checked with public employment agency," "checked with employer directly," "checked with friends or relatives," "placed or answered adds," "nothing," "other (specify)."

Such is the clarity of concept and reliability of measurement that goes into the determination of the unemployment rate, a statistic which makes politicians in office tremble and those out of office lick their chops. As with the Consumer Price Index, there is no deliberate falsification involved. Rather, the problem (thus far unsolved) is one of arriving at a rigorous definition, either of unemployment or of the price level, and then developing accurate tools of measurement to fit the definition.

THE MONEY SUPPLY

If the Consumer Price Index is a "monstrosity" and the unemployment rate an "abomination," then the money supply can only be described in words borrowed from Churchill: "a riddle, wrapped in enigma, surrounded by mystery." What is money? John Kenneth Galbraith, devoting an entire book to the subject, defines money as "what is commonly offered or received for the purchase of goods, services or other things."[5] He wisely avoids trying to measure it, for this definition does not describe anything that can be measured.

If one assumes for practical purposes that within the United States only dollars are money, then, what are dollars? Dollars include, of course, cash and checking accounts. How about savings accounts? With the development of so-called "now" accounts, giving individuals instant, convenient access to their savings, the distinction is already quite blurred. What about money market funds and even long-term bond funds, which allow shareholders to withdraw their money at any time simply by writing a check to the plumber? What is the role of credit cards as "money"?

To make matters worse, what about an Arab's dollar deposit in a London bank? That deposit can be used just as rapidly and effectively to snap up a choice piece of real estate as your or my deposit at Podunk National. Finally, what about marks, yen, and francs, any of which can be instantly converted into dollars for the purpose of bidding on that choice piece of real estate?

Even these few examples of "money" make the problems of concept and measurement associated with prices and unemployment seem like child's play by comparison. Yet, economists must try to measure money, because it is the supply of that money which largely determines the rate of inflation, and because the government, specifically our central bank, is supposed to control that supply.

The two most widely used measurements of the money supply are M1 (M standing for money), which is the sum of currency in circulation and checking accounts, and M2, which is currency, checking accounts and savings accounts in commercial banks. Beyond M1 and M2 there are at least a half dozen other published measurements of money, including such items as certificates of deposit, savings and loan deposits, "now" accounts, etc.* None of these measures, however, includes money market funds, credit card balances, or dollar deposits in overseas banks (Eurodollars). The world supply of money (dollars, marks, yen, and all other convertible currencies) is almost totally disregarded by American officialdom.

This book will be largely concerned with money and inflation, so the reader should be warned at the outset that the measurement of money has become one of the most intractable problems in the field of economics. There are no easy solutions and the hard ones haven't been found.

These complications hardly deter the press, pundits, and politicians. Every week changes in the "money supply"—M1 and M2—are published in the financial press. Wall Street pun-

---

*As this book goes to press the Federal Reserve Board has announced two new money measurements: M1 A and M1 B. Readers are advised to keep in daily touch through their newspapers regarding new and better official ways of measuring the money supply.

dits expatiate upon their significance. Financial markets react to them. Senators and congressmen regularly demand that the "monetary authorities" set targets for the growth of these numbers. The public attention given to the money supply illustrates a rule that is well-known to philosophers and divinity students: the less something can be understood, the more experts are to be found ready to interpret it. Among them, this writer.

GNP, the Consumer Price Index, overall unemployment, and the money supply are but a few of the hundreds or thousands of numerical series with which economists conjure to sell their services to industry and provide policy guidance to government. The conjuring process is called an "econometric model." The numbers, with accompanying equations, are fed into a computer. Out comes a prediction, and later a prescription, which is only as good as what went in.

This brief review of the numbers game is intended to dispel the layman's natural awe of anything that emerges from a computer. Obviously, one cannot talk about economic policy without sometimes mentioning numbers. But, virtually no set of numbers gives a completely accurate picture, and some numbers are far shakier than others. A few caveats may help the reader through the numbers maze:

In any forecast, small changes are probably meaningless. Large changes are grounds for close, if still skeptical, attention to the analysis or argument that the numbers have been advanced to justify.

At the high end of the reliability scale are the "old line" statistics, mostly published by the Commerce Department, of such series as Gross National Product, prices, wholesale and retail, and selected categories of unemployment. These have, in the words of a former Director of Research of the Federal Reserve Board, "a life of their own, apart from any individual's mind." At the lowest possible end are Treasury Department estimates of the tax revenues that will result from any tax change either proposed or opposed by the Administration in office. Such numbers are grinding a heavy political axe, and they also require assumptions about tax-payer behavior that are highly speculative. Though both kinds of numbers appear on government stationery, the credibility gulf between them is vast.

4

THE DEFICIT DILEMMA

We used to think that you could just spend your way out of a recession and increase employment by cutting taxes and boosting government spending. I tell you, in all candor, that that option no longer exists, and that insofar as it ever did exist, it only worked by injecting a bigger dose of inflation into the economy followed by a higher level of unemployment. That is the history of the past 20 years.

BRITISH PRIME MINISTER JAMES CALLAGHAN
addressing the Labor Party Congress September 1977

In order for a new idea to become a major religion, there are at least two requirements that must be met. One requirement is timing. The idea must appear to answer some deeply felt need of society at the time it emerges and for a long time thereafter. The second requirement is elusiveness—a blend of insight and obscurity. The idea must be so couched that while parts of it are crystal clear and inspirational, the rest is buried in an obscurity that can be interpreted only by an anointed priesthood. For it is this priesthood that will keep the religion alive.

Thus it has been with the Torah, the Bible, Das Kapital, and the General Theory of Employment, Interest, and Money, written in 1935 by the English economist, John Maynard Keynes.

Keynes' timing was perfect. The world was half a decade into the depths of a cruel depression from which there seemed no escape. The General Theory offered a comprehensive answer to everybody's prayers. Its message was simple, but the details were sufficiently shadowy to keep a vast and growing priesthood of economists busy interpreting them unto the third generation. For the last 35 years the label "economist" has been virtually synonymous with Keynesian, and even today most college students complete their economic course requirements only dimly aware of any alternative approaches to the solution of economic problems.

Prior to Keynes, most economic thought concentrated on the efficiency with which an economy functioned. The two villains were government intervention—through tariffs and subsidies—and business monopoly, for either one impaired the efficient functioning of the "free market." Depressions, which usually did not last very long, were relegated to the category of "acts of God." It was assumed that an economy naturally tended towards an equilibrium of full employment and maximum output, if government or monopoly didn't get in the way.

Keynes reasoned that under certain circumstances—notably, the circumstances prevailing in the 1930's—an economy could tend towards an equilibrium of substantial unemployment and stay there unless something were done about it. This could happen, according to Keynes, because at certain times people would consume less and save more than normal. If consumption fell, output would have to be cut back and employment would fall. Lower employment would in turn lead to still lower consumption and a downward spiral of economic activity. Thus, paradoxically, higher national saving could lead to lower national wealth.

The very notion that the virtues of saving could be carried too far flew in the face of Victorian morality, and conservatives have never forgiven Keynes his blasphemy. In a sense, Keynes was the intellectual watershed between the austere plateaus of the Victorian Age and the lush valleys of the Affluent Society.

His remedy was to stimulate consumption by providing more money to the relatively poor, who would automatically spend it. However, his was a more subtle approach than simple income redistribution. Instead of taking money from savers (the rich) and giving it to spenders (the poor), Keynes proposed that governments *borrow* some of the savers' savings and put this borrowed money into the hands of consumers, who could be counted upon to spend it. This is the meaning of a government budget deficit: The government spends more than it takes in through tax revenues and covers the difference by borrowing (from savers). The spending—on public works or welfare programs—increases consumption, as the people who receive this extra government money normally turn around and re-spend it immediately.

By proposing to *borrow* from savers rather than confiscate their savings outright through taxation, Keynes was being kind to the rich. He got little thanks for his kindness.

Once consumption had been increased in this fashion, Keynes and his followers reasoned that production and employment would rise, creating the need—and therefore the incentive—for new investment. Thus would the economy be pushed towards full employment.

This brief description is not intended to do justice to the subtleties of Keynes' writings, about which hundreds of acolytes have written thousands of books and articles. Rather, it is inteded to emphasize one major Keynesian contribution to the theory of economic policy: *You can stimulate an economy by transferring resources in the form of money (or food stamps, for that matter*) from savers to consumers.* This is called "fiscal stimulation." Conversely, the followers of Keynes imply that economic activity will be slowed by transferring resources back from consumers to savers. This is, theoretically, done by having a Federal Government budget surplus, and is called, by Keynesians, "fiscal drag."

It is important to remember that the essence of the matter is the transfer of resources from savers to consumers (or, rarely), from consumers to savers. Keynesians and critics of Keynes alike are usually apt to think only of the role of the Federal Government, with its budget deficit or surplus in this transfer process, but *the same transfers with the same effects on consumption and stimulation can and do take place outside of the Federal Government budget and in magnitudes that make that budget deficit pale into insignificance.* For the sake of brevity the transfer from saver to consumer will be called, henceforth, "Keynesian transfer."

Criticisms of this Keynesian recipe for restoration of full employment fall into two categories. The first is that government budget deficits cause inflation. The reasoning behind this criticism is that when government borrows to finance its deficit, the

---

*For the purposes of this chapter, the words "money" and "resources" are used interchangeably. Later on we will see that there is quite a difference between paper money and real resources.

cost of borrowing—interest rates—will rise throughout the economy unless the central bank makes cheap credit available.* Making cheap credit available causes inflation. There is some truth to this criticism, but, as shown in the next chapter, inflation can easily be created *without* a budget deficit.

The other major criticism of the Keynesian formula is that if the government drains savings in order to promote consumption, there will not be enough left for investment spending. The result will be gradual stagnation, much as a farm would stagnate if the farmer and his family ate up part of their seed grain each year. Closely allied to this criticism is a more subtle one: The very fact of large government budget deficits may undermine the confidence of those who must decide to invest in new factories that will raise output and employment. Keynes himself wrote, sixteen years before his General Theory, an elegant passage describing the ethics and outlook of an investment-rather than consumption-oriented society: 19th Century Europe:

> Europe was so organized socially and economically as to secure the maximum accumulation of capital. While there was some continuous improvement in the daily conditions of life of the mass of the population, Society was so framed as to throw a great part of the increased income into the control of the class least likely to consume it. The new rich of the nineteenth century were not brought up to large expenditures, and preferred the power investment gave them to the pleasures of immediate consumption. In fact, it was precisely the *inequality* of the distribution of wealth which made possible those vast accumulations of fixed wealth and of capital improvements which distinguished that age from all others. Herein lay, in fact, the main justification of the Capitalist System. If the rich had spent their new wealth on their own enjoyments, the world would long ago have found such a regimen intolerable. But like bees they saved and accumulated, not less to the advantage of the whole community because they themselves held narrower ends in prospect.
>
> The immense accumulations of fixed capital which, to the great benefit of mankind were built up during the half century before the war, could never have come about in a Society where wealth was divided equitably. The railways of the world, which that age

---

*Detailed discussion of interest rates and the role of the central bank will be found in the next chapter.

built as a monument to posterity, were, not less than the Pyramids
of Egypt, the work of labor which was not free to consume in
immediate enjoyment the full equivalent of its efforts.

Thus this remarkable system depended for its growth on a
double bluff or deception. On the one hand the laboring classes
accepted from ignorance and powerlessness, or were compelled,
persuaded, or cajoled by custom, convention, authority, and the
well-established order of Society into accepting a situation in
which they could call their own very little of the cake that they
and Nature and the capitalists were cooperating to produce. And
on the other hand the capitalist classes were allowed to call the
best part of the cake theirs and were theoretically free to consume
it, on the tacit underlying condition that they consumed very little
of it in practice. The duty of "saving" became nine-tenths of
virtue and the growth of the cake the object of true religion.
There grew round the non-consumption of the cake all those
instincts of puritanism which in other ages has withdrawn itself
from the world and has neglected the arts of production as well as
those of enjoyment. And so the cake increased; but to what end
was not clearly contemplated. Individuals would be exhorted not
so much to abstain as to defer, and to cultivate the pleasures of
security and anticipation. Saving was for old age or for your
children; but this was only theory—the virtue of the cake was that
it was never to be consumed, neither by you nor by your children
after you.[1]

We cannot and need not turn the clock that far back in order
to move the economy forward. But, some of the basic principles
of this account remain with us today. To survive and grow an
economy must maintain the *ability* to invest—by allowing for
adequate savings—and the *incentive* to invest—by maintaining
public confidence that investments once made will not be lost as
a result of government appropriation, taxation, regulation, or
economic mismanagement.

For all the mystique and controversy surrounding it, the
Keynesian doctrine, called "fiscal policy," was never given a
serious try until very recently. The New Deal stumbled along
with an unemployment rate of over 10 percent. According to
Keynesians, this was because the New Deal budget deficits were
not large enough. Also, in the dry words of an English Keynesian, "The rather wild collection of measures introduced by the
Roosevelt administration in 1933, when it came into office,

was obviously uninspired by any consistant doctrine."[2] Conservatives, of course, proclaimed that the New Deal proved fiscal policy to be a failure, but on that particular experience it is only fair to give the Keynesians the benefit of the doubt.

It was World War II that restored full employment.

As soon as the war was over, the followers of Keynes came into their own—and into the Government—in a big way. Scarred by memories of the Great Depression and inspired, doubtless, by King Canute, Congress legislated that henceforth there should never be unemployment in the land. Fiscal policy became the national economic religion. Its official high priests were the members of the President's Council of Economic Advisors. But it was Congress that held—and loosened—the deficit purse strings, though not much, because large deficits were simply not needed in the postwar prosperity. Of the twenty years between 1947 and 1966, twelve were deficit and eight were surplus. In only one year—1959, during a Republican Administration—was the deficit in excess of $10 billion. Most of the larger deficits were in fact the result of lagging tax revenues rather than deliberate policy. None had a demonstrable impact on the economy one way or another.

For, these were the bountiful years when the world's economy leapt ahead, fueled by cheap energy, new technology, and the momentum of postwar recovery. This did not deter the Keynesian economists, who were shaping government policy, from taking full credit for the prosperity and progress which continued about them. Like children on the airplane ride at an amusement park they proudly twirled their cockpit steering wheels, believing that they themselves were making the planes fly. Listen to their gleeful cries:

It is no accident that this most successful period of sustained growth in our economic history has coincided with a new determination to apply economic policies in active pursuit of the goals of the Employment act.

GARDNER ACKLEY, *Economic Report of the President, 1968*

The vigorous and unbroken expansion of the last eight years is in dramatic contrast to the 30 month average duration (of expansion) of previous years. No longer is the performance of the

Like children on an airplane ride

American economy generally interpreted in terms of stages of the business cycle. No longer do we consider periodic recessions once every 3 or 4 years an inevitable fact of life.

ARTHUR OKUN, *Economic Report of the President, 1969*

When the priesthood takes too much credit for rainfall, it might just get the blame when drought rolls around. By 1968 and 1969 drought was on the way.

After an extremely bumpy ride through gusts of inflation between 1968 and 1974, the world's economy hit the ground in 1975 with its worst depression since the 1930's. It thus fell to a Republican Administration to give Keynes his first real chance. In fiscal 1976, the Federal Government budget deficit hit $65 billion. Congress did its bit by enacting two successive tax cuts for lower income brackets to stimulate consumption. This time it could not be claimed that the deficits were not large enough for a fair test!

The test results? Mixed. The last half of the 1970's could best be described as a successful Keynesian depression. After an initial sharp rise, unemployment was rapidly brought down. Consumer demand kept output and employment humming along. The cruelty and despair of the Great Depression were largely avoided.

In this sense, Keynes' recipe was a success. The depression was made comfortable. But how long could this last? The nation's rate of investment slumped and productivity declined. By now growth has reached a standstill. Reasons for this *malaise* are many, including government policies that have nothing to do with the budget deficit, such as regulatory and energy incoherence. But, the budget deficit itself may have tended to preempt savings which otherwise would have gone into investment. Furthermore, the public attention paid to the Federal Government deficit emphasizes the impression that our government cannot control itself.

This attention may be misplaced. Newspaper headlines, and the proposed constitutional amendment to require a balanced budget, concentrate on the Federal Government. However, as we all know, we also have state and city governments. The state and local governments, in recent years, have been running *surpluses* in their annual budgets, due entirely to money that they get from the Federal Government. Therefore, we must look not at the Federal deficit alone, but at the total deficits of Federal, state and local governments. For example, in 1977, when the Federal Government had a budget deficit of a horrendous $48 billion, state and local governments collectively ran a surplus of $30 billion, bringing the total government deficit to a more manageable, and less headline-grabbing, $18 billion. In 1978, state and local surpluses just about offset the Federal deficit, and in 1979 they exceeded it. The following table tells the story for the past decade:

Year	Federal Deficit[a]	State and Local Government Surplus[a]	Net Deficit or Surplus[a]	Rate of Inflation (%)
1970	−12.1	2.8	−9.4	5.9
1971	−22.0	3.7	−18.3	4.3
1972	−17.3	13.7	−3.5	3.3
1973	−6.7	13.0	6.3	6.2
1974	−10.7	7.6	−3.2	11.0
1975	−70.6	6.2	−64.4	9.1
1976	−53.6	17.9	−35.7	5.8
1977	−46.3	26.8	−19.5	6.5
1978	−27.7	27.4	−0.3	9.9
1979	−10.5	24.4	13.9	13.1

[a]Source: Economic Report of the President, 1980, Table B-72.

These figures scarcely support the widely held contention that government deficits cause inflation.

Once the government deficit is reduced to its real magnitude—$64 billion in 1975 and $33 billion the year after, but otherwise always below $20 billion—it becomes a small element in the total scheme of Keynesian transfers.

It will be remembered that the essence of fiscal policy is the transfer of resources from savers to consumers by having the government borrow from savers and turn the money over to consumers. As Keynes succinctly phrased his recipe, "I lay overwhelming emphasis on the increase in national purchasing power resulting from government expenditures financed by loans."[2] What many people, pro-Keynes or anti-Keynes, may have forgotten or may never have realized, is that these similar transfers are taking place outside the framework of the government budget.

The first of these transfers is the annual increase in consumer installment debt. This debt increased by $44 billion in 1978. Why should this be lumped in with the Government deficit? Because, the process is the same and the effects are the same. In the case of a government budget deficit, savers buy government bonds or put their money in banks, which buy government bonds. The government turns the money over to consumers who spend it. In the case of consumer debt, the banks lend the money that savers have deposited with them to consumers. The only difference is that the government is not involved.

But, the increase in consumer *installment* debt is only part of the larger Keynesian transfer. Recently, *residential mortgage debt has been increasing by about $100 billion each year.* Again, it is the banks that take savers' money and relend this money to consumers by financing the purchases of houses or financing other purchases based on the increased market value of houses already owned. What is the difference between the government going into debt to provide food stamps to a welfare family which will then have enough cash to buy a television set, a blue collar family going into debt to buy a car, and a rising executive raising his mortgage to finance a sailboat, a vacation, or a divorce? Each of these operations means going into debt, in other words tapping someone else's savings, in order to finance consumption. Each drains the resources that would otherwise be available for investment. Each borrows from the future, like the farm family eating its seed grain.

Compared with a government deficit that reached a historical maximum of $64 billion in only one year, the regular yearly increases in consumer borrowing—installment plus mortgage—are running at $150 billion! It is an old cliché that every family has to balance its budget, and therefore the government should do the same. What is going on today would suggest that this cliché is *passé.* American families are as a whole not balancing their budgets, and the American banking system seems only too happy to accommodate these family budget deficits.

There is a final, larger dimension to the savings-consumption-investment question, a dimension that offers considerable hope for the future. This is the *international dimension.* Thus far, we have been tacitly assuming a fixed pool each year of national savings that are either invested or are diverted in part to consumption. However, American savers are not the only savers who buy U.S. Government bonds or put their money in American banks. Also, strange to say, our government is not the only government which levies taxes on us. Chapter 1 recalled a meeting of economists convened by the newly inaugurated President Ford in early September 1974. One of the very few of those attending who warned of a serious recession was Professor Richard Cooper of Yale University, now Undersecretary of State for Economic Affairs. He suggested that the United States and Saudi Arabian government budget deficits be viewed as a consolidated whole. This remark, a rather sophisticated one, was largely ignored, but by now it is generally accepted that higher OPEC prices for oil have the same effect that a U.S. Government tax on oil would have—a "fiscal drag" to use Keynesian terminology.* The only difference is that the Arabs use some of their "tax" proceeds to buy U.S. Government bonds, whereas if the tax on oil were levied by the U.S. Government directly, the bonds would not have had to be issued in the first place.

This may sound at first like a rather complicated new idea sprung on the reader, but it is only an internationalized application of the savings-consumption principle set forth earlier: If the U.S. government were to tax oil sales and thereby have a budget *surplus,* the net effect would be to lower American consumption and make more money available for investment. If, instead, the *Arabs* raise oil prices, money is also taken away from the consumer and is potentially available for investment (less the amounts which the Arabs themselves spend on consumption). Some of this money is already being reinvested in America; much more could be. Arab "savings" range from $50 to $100 billion each year.

In addition to these OPEC savings, there are the savings that are accruing in Europe and Japan. Much has been made of the

---

*See also William C. Cates, "The $70 billion Excise Tax," *Euromoney,* September 1974.

fact that the savings rate in Europe and Japan is substantially higher than that in the United States. What is forgotten in this lament is that savings need not be invested in the country in which they are made. The United States itself was a heavy exporter of capital during the 1950's and 1960's, indeed, in amounts frequently larger than our government budget deficits. There is no reason why it cannot become an equally heavy *importer* of capital, which would, of course, add to that pool of domestic savings available for investment in American factories, machinery, and technology.

A stronger dollar and a rising stock market would be a powerful magnet to foreign investors, from Arab sheiks to Zurich gnomes. With all its faults, this country offers the safest investment haven in the world. Any changes in government policy which served to make investment in American industry, by foreigners as well as Americans, more attractive would bring about an inflow of capital to this country that would make past, present, or future government budget deficits appear insignificant. This is a compelling argument for a well-designed tax cut.

SUMMARY

1. The idea of fiscal policy is to stimulate the economy by transferring resources (money) from savers to consumers. The government does this by having a budget deficit, thus borrowing from savers and distributing the proceeds to consumers.
2. This kind of stimulation-through-consumption may be useful for short periods, and, indeed, it is sometimes inevitable when there is an economic downturn which reduces tax receipts and simultaneously increases claims on the government for unemployment insurance and welfare.
3. However, over longer periods of time, this transfer from savers to consumers is bound to result in lower investment and gradual economic stagnation.
4. The government budget deficits of the 1970's may help to explain the decline in investment and growth during this decade. However, there are other explanations, including the uncertainties surrounding government regulatory policies coupled with the lack of a clear energy policy.

Inflation itself has increased the desire to consume and decreased the willingness to save and invest.

5. The government budget deficit has been a relatively small factor in the total transfer of resources between savers and consumers. Constant yearly increases in consumer debt have been much more important. So has the international dimension, where the OPEC oil exporters emerge as a major offset to domestic fiscal policy. These countries, in effect, "tax" American consumers and use part of these tax proceeds to buy U.S. Government bonds and otherwise invest in this country.

6. In addition to OPEC money, the savings of other developed countries are already flowing into the United States as investment capital. If government followed policies that made this country an even more attractive place to invest in, the flow of these foreign savings could increase dramatically.

7. Compared with yearly increases in consumer debt and with the present and potential ebb and flow of foreign-owned money across our borders, the amount of the government budget deficit is not very significant. For this reason, concentration on eliminating the budget deficit as a goal in itself is misplaced. The United States could, for example, well afford tax cuts designed to make investment in American business more attractive, even if these cuts temporarily increased the budget deficit.

8. There is little evidence that budget deficits *per se* cause inflation. As a matter of fact, economic policy-makers have discovered a quicker and more direct way to create inflation: just print money.

5

MONEY TERROR

In its 65-year history, to the best of my knowledge, the Federal
Reserve Board has never admitted error in any official statement.

MILTON FRIEDMAN
Newsweek, July 24, 1978

In a parable told by Milton Friedman, Nobel Laureate and
dean of the "Monetarist" school of economists, an airplane flew
over a small country in the dead of night, dropping packets of
currency—enough to double the country's money supply. During the ensuing days, as they discovered these currency notes,
the lucky citizens congratulated themselves and proceeded to
spend most of their new money. Retail sales boomed and the
pace of production quickened. Eventually, however, with all the
extra money being spent on them, goods and services rose in
price until they were about double what they had been. Economic activity settled back to where it had been before, because
the only net effect of the airdrop had been to double the supply
and therefore halve the value of the country's currency.[1]
   A slight change in that story produces a very different result.
Suppose the President of the United States one day announces
that any citizen owning dollars in cash or in a bank account will
receive, free, one new dollar bill for each dollar he already
holds. The instant effect is a doubling of prices, as everyone
realizes that two dollars are now worth what one dollar had
been worth the day before. No one would have any reason to
feel one whit richer than he had felt before or to spend any
more than he had been spending.

The first of these examples describes an officially sanctioned con game known as "money illusion" which governments play when they deliberately inflate the money supply to stimulate the economy. So long as people are not conscious that the amount of money is increasing—and therefore its value dropping—they will feel personally more prosperous as their wages and salaries rise, and they will tend to spend most of the increase in their incomes. However, as Abraham Lincoln pointed out, not even a government con game can go on forever.

The reelection of President Nixon in 1972 may well have been the last time that the game of "money illusion" was successfully played by the United States Government. Price controls were in force, so that the visible symptoms of inflation were suppressed. Beneath this convenient lid, the Federal Reserve System boiled the pot by printing* an unprecedented amount of money, which found its way into the pockets of happy consumers and voters. Only in 1973–1974, aided by sharp increases in food and oil prices, did all the new money produce a wave of inflation followed by a spasm of contraction in 1975. The public found itself badly burned, and the age of monetary innocence came to an end. Things will never be quite the same again.

It should be obvious from even so brief an outline that monetary stimulation works only through deception. This is a truism which most politicians do not understand and, after Watergate, would scarcely care to acknowledge. Instead, the political demand is for open guidelines, openly arrived at. Many members of Congress think that the monetary authorities, meaning the Federal Reserve Board, should set high monetary targets and announce them in advance, after debating them in the fishbowl of full publicity.

This sounds comfortingly like the "American way" of doing things, but in practice such a policy operates—with one disastrous difference—just like the second story, wherein a free

---

*Strictly speaking, money is only "printed" by the Bureau of Printing and Engraving and the Mint. What the Fed does is to allow bank deposits to expand, a process which will be described in this chapter. However, even former Fed Chairman, G. William Miller, used the verb "print" to describe the organization's money creation. It is a vivid verb and deserves to be used from time to time.

extra dollar is proclaimed for everybody. Suppose there is an
official announcement that the money supply will be increased
by 20% during the next year. Public reaction will be one of
instant anticipation of the promised event. Prices will be
marked up wherever possible, and labor will demand wage increases to compensate for the anticipated rise in the cost of
living. The disastrous difference between this announcement
of a 20% increase in the money supply and the hypothetical
proclamation of an extra dollar for everybody is that only those
who can claim protection against inflation through wage and
price markups will be able to stay even. Those who have savings
in the bank and those who are on fixed incomes or who await
fixed pensions know only that their savings, incomes, and pensions will decline some 20% in buying power.* The psychological impact can best be described as "money terror." Some consumers buy in anticipation of the price rises that will surely
follow. Others, seeing their nest eggs dwindling, retrench and
actually hoard cash. (During the worst periods of inflation, public holdings of cash have, paradoxically, increased.)

Meanwhile, the same politicians who demanded high monetary targets—publicly proclaimed—to stimulate the economy
will excoriate the inevitably resulting price increases as "administered pricing" and will wonder dimly why the economy is
not being stimulated. Special Presidential representatives will
be appointed to jawbone the public, meaning business and
labor leaders, to hold prices and wages in line.

Finally, much to everybody's confusion, interest rates will
rise, putting a crimp in housing activity, the stock market, and
new investment. This rise in interest rates, which attends the
printing of too much paper money, is the most confusing and
disappointing phenomenon of all, because, according to time-
honored economic theory, creating more money is supposed to
lower interest rates. After all, the more money there is, the less it
should cost. Right?

Wrong. The interest rate—the amount that is charged for

*To be precise, the decline in buying power will be 20%, *less* the percentage growth in
"real" or physical output of goods and services. According to monetary theory, if the
economy grows at 3% a year, for example, then a 3% growth in the money supply
would produce no inflation. Assuming the same 3% real growth, a 20% money supply
increase would only reduce the value of the currency by 17%.

money lent—is the sum of three elements or considerations: 1) the credit-worthiness of the borrower, 2) the demand for credit in the economy (in booms this is high; in busts it is low), and 3) public anticipation of what the money lent will be worth in terms of goods that can be purchased once the loan is repaid. Before I lend you $100 for a year I must first calculate whether you will pay me back, then whether there are other borrowers who might pay me more and, finally, what the buying-power of that $100 will be when I do get it back. If the government has already indicated that it will print so much paper money that prices may be 20% higher at the end of the year, then even a 20% interest rate will net me nothing for your use of my money. However, if I try to get 20% or more, voices will be heard throughout the land accusing me of usury, administered interest rates, and generally antisocial behavior.

Voices will also be heard wondering in bewilderment why a policy of generous money-printing, specifically designed to maintain low interest rates, ended up producing high interest rates. Then a curious thing will happen: the very people who, at the urging of Congress, printed all the money designed to produce low interest rates, will be blamed for a "tight money policy" because their actions in fact produced high interest rates.

These people are our central bankers. They wear the mantles of impeccable central bank conservatism, yet, since the early 1970's they have made an astonishing contribution to the inflation which has robbed millions of Americans of their savings and which is destroying the economies and institutions of the Western World. They are the members of the Federal Reserve Board, or "Fed" for short. To understand how and why the Fed has done this, one must look at how it operates, and distinguish what it *can* do from what people, including some of its own officials, *think* it can do.

A central bank is a "bankers' bank." Commercial banks can borrow from it, but also must keep part of their own money—so-called "reserves"—deposited with it. (Unfortunately, this does not include all commercial banks, just those who are members of the Federal Reserve System, some 5,800 of them.) These reserves are the fulcrum of whatever control the Fed has over the amount of money created in this country. A member bank must keep about 12½% of its customers' deposits as a reserve with the Fed. Commercial banks are in business to make money. To do this they try to make as many loans as they can. Each loan creates a deposit, for if you borrow from your bank, the bank opens an account for you, which is a deposit. If you pay off a creditor with the bank loan, then he gets a deposit in the same or another bank. Bank deposits, being as good as cash in your wallet, are money. Deposits, and therefore the supply of money, tend to expand just as far as the reserve requirements will allow. Each bank with reserves at the Fed of $100 million will strive to have deposits of $800 million, the maximum allowed by the legal reserve requirement.

The reserve requirement thus acts as a leash by which the Fed controls the banking system dog. The Fed can give the leash a sharp jerk by raising (or lowering) reserve requirements, and this it does from time to time. But mostly it nudges the dog along on a daily basis by increasing or decreasing the reserves themselves. This is done, oddly enough, by trading in Treasury bills. One of the largest and most active markets in the world is the New York money market. Each day billions of dollars worth of Treasury bills, bonds, commercial paper, and other "debt instruments" are traded over the telephone by commercial banks for their own and their customers' accounts, by corporations and by dealers who specialize in such trading. The Fed is also active in this market, usually dealing in Treasury bills and usually through the dealers. When the Fed buys Treasury bills from a commercial bank, the account of that bank with the Fed is credited. This adds to the reserves that the bank has with the Fed and lets the bank expand its deposits. In the opposite direction, if the Fed sells Treasury bills to a bank, the bank pays for them out of its reserves with the Fed, and must either contract its deposits by making no more loans, or borrow reserves from other banks or from the Fed itself.

The very process of buying and selling Treasury bills in the New York money market gives rise to a dangerous misconception concerning the Fed's powers. This is the idea that the Fed can control interest rates. When the Fed buys Treasury bills heavily, their price goes up, the atmosphere of the entire money market improves, and interest rates fall. When the Fed sells, bill prices go down and therefore interest rates rise. This gives Fed officials a wonderful sense of power, but that power is, if not illusory, at least temporary. For, each time the Fed buys Treasury bills it is expanding bank reserves. After a while bank deposits—the major component of the money supply—expand. As soon as the public gets wind of this expansion in the money supply, money terror—the anticipation of inflation—sets in, and interest rates *rise*.

On a day-to-day trading basis in the New York money market, the Fed is the biggest boy on the block: when the Fed buys, prices rise, which means interest rates fall. When it sells, prices fall; interest rates rise. This causes Wall Street pundits to say that the Fed has "eased" credit and lowered interest rates, in the first case, or "tightened" credit and raised them, in the second. But, the block is not the whole city, and the later effect—sometimes months later—is usually the opposite of what was intended. When people see that the money supply is rising, lenders will be willing to put out their money only at higher interest rates, while borrowers become eager to pay these rates in order to buy gold, commodity futures, real estate, and foreign currencies anything to escape the declining value of the dollar. Thus, the final effect on interest rates of the Fed's actions in buying or selling Treasury bills is exactly the opposite of the initial, intended effect.

This perverse, unintended relationship between money creation and interest rates is a fact that will have to be understood by economists, by the public, and by politicians before this nation ever rids itself of the curse of inflation. So long as people believe that printing money lowers interest rates and stimulates the economy, they will demand that the Fed print more money—and create more inflation—each time that interest rates rise. Fortunately, the new Chairman of the Fed apparently does understand this relationship. Shortly after his appointment, Paul Volcker told the press that even if the Fed "exploded the money supply" interest rates would "go up" rather than down.[2]

However, such are the political pressures in a democracy that the Fed cannot for long act by itself. The Federal Reserve is an independent body, but it was created by Congress and it is responsible to Congress. Even if, for once, it goes in the right direction, it cannot stray too far from the fold of political consensus. It will not be an easy task to make political consensus face the facts. Generations of Americans have grown up believing, when they thought about it, that the central bank controls interest rates, printing money to make them go down and restraining money creation to make them rise. This belief was founded on money illusion, which worked nicely up through the 1960's. But, today we live in the age of money terror and the rules are reversed.

When the Fed is not seeking to control interest rates, it tries to regulate the money supply. The money supply, it will be remembered, is made up of cash and bank deposits, with demand deposits included in M1 and time deposits in M2. Increasing bank reserves enables these deposits to expand, decreasing bank reserves forces them to contract.

Bank reserves, coupled with currency in circulation and bank vaults, are known as the "monetary base," a rather wobbly base upon which an enormous pyramid of money sits precariously. The base is wobbly, because the Fed only has control over a small part of it. As of mid 1979, the monetary base amounted to $148 billion, of which $102 billion was currency in circulation, $13 billion cash in bank vaults, and only $33 billion reserves deposited by member banks with the Fed. The Fed has no control over the amount of currency in circulation: that is already in wallets, under mattresses, or busy paying for dope smuggled into the country. Banks do not keep any more cash in their vaults than absolutely necessary, because this cash pays no interest. The only magnitude that is under the Fed's control is the $33 billion of bank reserves. On top of the controllable base of $33 billion sits the money pyramid: $375 billion of M1 or $925 billion of M2.

The Fed's job is not easy, but the Fed's leadership has not made things any easier for itself. Early in 1978 I was told by a top Fed official that no one at the Fed on a senior level ever paid any attention to the monetary base. *The only statistic over which the Fed has direct control was not considered worth looking at.*

What the Fed *does* look at, in addition to interest rates, are the "monetary aggregates," M1 and M2. When these zoom up-

Like a kid with a yo-yo

wards, the Fed starts selling Treasury bills; when they fail to grow in line with preset targets announced in Congressional testimony, the Fed moves to increase reserves by buying Treasury bills. The process makes one think of a kid with a yo-yo, who automatically moves his hand down when the yo-yo gets too high and up again when the yo-yo nears its low point. The yo-yo, upon which the kid's eye is fixed, is the money supply; the hand is the monetary base. This technique is splendid for playing with yo-yos, but hardly suitable for building confidence in a currency.

Each upward surge in M1 and M2 causes shivers of money terror throughout not only the nation but the world. Financial markets fall, the dollar falls, and the price of gold makes new highs. As Milton Friedman has pointed out repeatedly, bad as a high rate of money increase is, the swoops and dives produced by the Fed are even worse.

To recapitulate, the inflation of the past decade has ushered in the Age of Money Terror. In this Age some of the ideas upon which most economists grew up, and which non-economists simply assumed, are no longer valid.

1. The thesis that creating more money will lower interest rates and stimulate output and employment no longer holds water. In order for it to be valid, "money illusion" must be present, i.e., people must believe that the extra dollars they are getting are not declining in value.

2. Even the belief that the Fed can effectively control the money supply may be suspect. The Fed has direct influence only over a very small base of reserves—$33 billion—upon which a very large pyramid of bank deposits—$925 billion—is perched.

Money terror also has an international dimension. The breaking, in 1971, of the link between the dollar and gold has contributed mightily to the public loss of confidence in the dollar and in many other currencies. So has the system of floating exchanges rates. Inflation is a worldwide phenomenon.

6

INTERNATIONAL
MONEY TERROR

It is good to remember that no paper money can serve as a stable
measure or store of value.

STANISLAV M. MENSHIKOV
Soviet Economist at the United Nations, 1978

Since 1973 the world has been on a floating exchange rate
system, which means that most major currencies are traded
back and forth at prices that may change in either direction
from day to day and even from minute to minute. Every
traveler over the past five years has had the unsettling experience of receiving two German marks for a dollar on Tuesday
but only 1.85 marks on Wednesday. He curses himself for not
having changed more money on Tuesday. Arriving in England
on Thursday he finds that pounds cost $2.25 each. The follow-
ing Monday they can be had for $2.10.

The relationship between paper currencies, with their fluc-
tuations and gyrations, boil down to nothing more mysterious
than the law of supply and demand: if too much money is
printed, its value will fall abroad just as it falls at home.

This can be illustrated by the story of two mythical countries,
Illusia and Spartica. The Illusians were activists. Whatever the
state of their economy, they believed that it could—and therefore must—be made better by government action. The Sparti-
cans tended to "take what comes" and make the best of it. Their
currencies were called, respectively, the illy and the spart, and,
as our story begins, one illy equaled one spart.

One day the chairman of the central bank of Illusia, wishing to lower interest rates, promote full employment, and finance the Illusian government deficit, set out to create money with the intent to double Illusia's money supply in a year's time. This caused Illusian prices to rise, while the foreign exchange value of the illy floated downwards. By the time most people were aware of what the central bank chairman was doing, it took two illies to buy one spart. And, the illy kept sinking in value, because no one was sure that the central bank chairman, in his enthusiasm,would stop at simply doubling the money supply.*

At the same time interest rates rose in Illusia, which was exactly contrary to the good intentions of the Illusian central bank chairman. Lenders demanded higher interest rates to compensate themselves for the loss in value of the illy, while borrowers were willing to pay the higher rates so that they could turn around and buy sparts. This was known as getting one's money out of the country.

Due to the high interest rates, and a sharp fall in the Illusian stock market which accompanied them, production stagnated and unemployment rose.

This story describes much of what has been happening in the world during the 1970's. Indiscriminate money creation caused the Italian lire to fall sharply in 1975 and the British pound to do the same in 1976. The American dollar has suffered from overprinting throughout the decade. In none of these countries has money printing produced any visible benefit.

If excessive money creation has such disastrous results, why do central bankers still engage in "monetary stimulation"? Why

---

*Two top economists in what might loosely be called the "Rational Expectations" school of economic thought have recently made significant contributions to the theory of exchange rate movements. Dr. Michael W. Keran, Director of Research of the Federal Reserve Bank of San Francisco, concludes, with a thorough demonstration, that " . . . an important share of the exchange rate movements of the dollar against key foreign currencies can be explained by monetary factors, rather than by speculation or changes in such real factors as the terms of trade."[1]
Professor Neil Wallace of the University of Minnesota has arrived at a somewhat different and very interesting conclusion. He believes that a system of floating rates between fiat (i.e., paper) currencies inevitably makes the determination of a proper, or "equilibrium," price for each currency impossible. To put his argument in a nutshell, nobody can possibly figure out the relative values of things (in this case, currencies) that themselves have no intrinsic value.[2] The practical implication of Professor Wallace's proposition is that free-floating exchange markets will inevitably be unstable and vulnerable to psychological pressures. This point will come up again at the end of Chapter 7.

did such luminaries as Senator Proxmire and Congressman Reuss and Professors Walter Heller and Arthur Okun, former Chairmen of the President's Council of Economic Advisors, argue repeatedly during the decade for an "expansive money supply"? The answer is probably that their thinking was formed in an earlier age, before floating exchange rates entered the picture.

This earlier age included two suberas: (1) the era of the Gold Standard, which flourished in Europe in the 18th and 19th centuries and ended for most countries with the onset of World War I, and (2) the post-World War II era of the Gold Exchange Standard, which lasted until August 15, 1971. (The interwar period was an unpleasant hiatus of mixed standards.)

Under the Gold Standard, the monies of all major nations could be exchanged for a commodity, gold, that was in limited supply. This linkage to gold gave money a value of its own in the public mind. It also set very definite limits to the amount of abuse to which money could be subjected by central bankers.

Back to Illusia and Spartica to explain how the nineteenth century Gold Standard worked. Under the Gold Standard, the banking systems of both Illusia and Spartica were based on reserves of gold. If bank lending expanded in Illusia, either because of the policies of the central bank chairman or because of the normal rhythm of business activity, then prices rose. This made exports more expensive and imports cheaper. Illusians bought cheaper Spartican goods and paid for them with gold, which flowed from Illusia to Spartica. The outflow of gold from Illusia soon forced a contraction of lending by Illusian banks; the inflow of gold into Spartica made that country's bank reserves expand. Bank lending rose in Spartica, and pretty soon prices rose as well. Eventually the flow of gold from Illusia to Spartica stopped or reversed. In this fashion, the back and forth flow of gold between the two countries maintained price equilibrium between them, much as the level of water remains the same between two tanks connected by a tube.

People believed in gold, and most of the time they believed in their currencies, which were based on gold.

The Gold Exchange Standard after World War II worked in much the same way, except that the dollar became a substitute for gold. At the end of the War, the United States held most of the world's gold, and this gold was the backing for the dollar.

Other countries were content to hold gold-backed dollars, because the United States was willing at any time to exchange dollars held by the central bank of any other country for gold. Dollars that could be exchanged for gold were—at least in theory—as good as gold. Such was the nature and meaning of the Gold Exchange Standard, which worked very well until it was abused.

For the first fifteen years after the War dollars were in short supply. Indeed, much of the economic literature of that time dealt with the "dollar shortage." So long as the dollar was a relative rarity, no nation needed to question the gold guarantee that supported it. Of course a few did, for Europeans have a sense of history and a degree of skepticism that is lacking in the New World. Individual countries quietly exchanged some of their dollars each year for gold.

The Gold Exchange Standard worked like the Gold Standard, but with one assymetrical exception. In every nation other than the United States, the dollar was used for reserves as if it were gold. If an inflation took place in France, for example, the French treasury would lose dollar reserves, the dollars flowing to Germany, Japan, and even back to the United States. The outflow of dollar reserves would contract economic activity in France, just as the loss of gold under the Gold Standard led to economic contraction. This was called the "discipline" of the balance of payments.

However, if the United States overexpanded, there was no contraction necessary. Dollars flowing out of the United States could be replaced, as it were, simply by printing extra dollars. The reserves of other countries expanded without any comparable contraction in the United States. It was this assymmetry and its abuse by the Federal Reserve Board that finally broke up the Gold Exchange Standard.

Under the Gold and Gold Exchange Standards, exchange rates between most currencies were "fixed," that is, travelers and traders could go to sleep each night confident that a dollar would buy just as many marks or pounds on the morrow as it had that day. Weekends, however, were another matter. For, even under fixed exchange rates, nations could and did devalue their currencies, a policy lurch usually carried out on the Sabbath, when the financial markets were closed.

The difference between fixed and floating rates is not absolute. In our first example, when the chairman of the central bank of Illusia decided to stimulate the economy by doubling the money supply, the illy floated down until it took two or more illies to buy one spart. Under fixed rates the scenario would be somewhat different but the result the same. As more money circulated around in Illusia, prices would rise, imports would rise, and exports would fall. Sensing the trend, citizens of both Illusia and Spartica would take all the illies they had and buy sparts at the rate of one spart for one illy. Spartican exporters would demand payment in sparts. Illusian exporters would also try to get payment in sparts. This is called "speculative pressure" and canny citizens who figure out what's going on are called, pejoratively, "speculators." The Spartican central bank would obviously end up with a lot of illies and would then demand gold from the Illusian central bank in exchange for them. Seeing itself about to run out of reserves, the Illusian Government would solemnly pledge never to devalue the illy, at the same time denouncing speculators. The following Sabbath the illy would be devalued by half, or perhaps more than half in order to quiet the speculation. Such was the manner in which Britain devalued the pound in 1949 and 1967 and France the franc in 1957, 1958, and 1969.

Thus, when exchange rates are fixed, a country that starts to run out of reserves either must submit to the "discipline of the balance of payments," allowing its economy to contract, or it must devalue. Under floating rates, the currency just floats down as domestic prices rise. The result is the same, yet there is a very important psychological difference. Devaluation is—or used to be—politically unpopular, a confession of failure by the devaluing government. Therefore, at least for long periods, the people in countries that had fixed exchange rates were able to have confidence in their currencies, whose values were stable from day to day. Furthermore, under the Gold Exchange Standard, there was a link via the dollar to gold. However tenuous, this link to gold was probably an important factor in the public confidence enjoyed by most currencies most of the time during the 1950's and early 1960's. The dollar was nearly sacrosanct. It never had to be devalued. If too many were printed, other countries were still eager to gobble them up.

This stability lent meaning to the phrase "sound as a dollar."

While it was customary to complain about inflation, inflationary expectations, in the extreme sense in which we know them today, did not exist. Some prices might be rising, but the dollar was not falling. This stable situation with the absence of inflationary expectations—or money terror—had important implications for interest rates and for economists' perceptions of monetary policy. As was pointed out in the last chapter, interest rates are determined by three factors: risk that the borrower might go bankrupt, demand for credit, and expectation of inflation. If inflationary expectations are minimal, then it is quite reasonable to assume that an "easy money" policy could lower interest rates, stimulate lending and business activity. This is, in fact, what happened during the fixed rate era: easy money in one country would produce lower interest rates and an increase in lending. It would also, however, cause funds to move to other countries in search of higher interest rates.

So long as the easy money policy originated in the United States, it could continue unchecked. American prices and imports would rise; exports would fall. At the same time, people holding dollars would buy marks, francs, and yen in search of higher interest rates. The United States ran a balance of payments deficit and other countries accumulated dollars. All that the economists responsible for American policy saw, however, was that easy money in the United States produced lower interest rates and, perhaps, economic expansion, with some nasty and dimly understood problem called the balance of payments lurking in the wings. One way to deal with this inexplicable balance of payments problem was to levy a special tax on Americans who moved their money abroad in search of higher interest rates. On July 18, 1963 the Administration announced an "Interest Equalization Tax" on the movement of money abroad. Unfortunately, this kind of band-aid was powerless to stave off the ultimate collapse of the Gold Exchange Standard.

While the system lasted, however, it was beautiful for America. Easy money produced lower interest rates and higher economic activity with no pain. We exported our excess dollars, and for a long time the entire world prospered. This is the era in which most of the economists and politicians who today make policy in the United States were trained, which explains why they continue to advocate what today is the height of folly. For, ever since the collapse of the Gold Exchange Standard, easy money has produced only higher interest rates and economic stagnation.

The effects of excess money creation on an individual country and its neighbors can now be summarized: under the Gold Standard, the Gold Exchange Standard, and Floating Rates. The rules of the Gold Standard applied under the Gold Exchange Standard to all countries except the United States. All of these other countries were obliged to worry about their dollar balances as if those dollars were gold. They, but not the United States, were subject to the "discipline of the balance of payments."

A. GOLD STANDARD
   1. Illusian central bank chairman increases the money supply.
   2. Prices and imports rise; exports fall. Interest rates fall.
   3. Money flows to Spartica to pay for imports and in search of higher interest rates.
   4. Illusia loses reserves and must allow its economy to contract, *or*
   5. Illusia devalues.

B. GOLD EXCHANGE STANDARD (with the Illy as the reserve currency)
   1. Illusian central bank chairman increases the money supply.
   2. Prices and imports rise; exports fall.
   3. Interest rates fall.
   4. Money flows to Spartica to pay for imports and in search of higher interest rates.
   5. Spartica's reserves of illies rise, and the Illusian inflation spreads to Spartica.
   6. Spartica asks for a little gold from time to time but is otherwise content to hold illies as part of its reserves.
   7. Illusian economic policy-makers conclude that they're onto a good thing and keep printing money until Spartica refuses to accept any more paper illies.
     This causes the system to collapse, leading to . . . .

C. FLOATING RATES
   1. Illusian central bank chairman increases the money supply.

2. Prices rise.

3. Interest rates rise, as money terror (inflationary expectation) grips both the domestic population and foreign creditors.

4. Business activity stagnates and employment drops.

5. Central bank chairman retires with his reputation intact as an inflation-fighter who has created high interest rates, *or*

6. Central bank chairman tries to get things under control and is promptly chastized by "liberal" economists and politicians who can only remember how nice it used to be under the Gold Exchange Standard. President of Illusia promises to produce a new central bank chairman every four years, or more often if the incumbent learns too fast.

With this analytical framework it is now possible to explore the anatomy of a government economic policy, in this case probably the most far-reaching policy seen in our generation: the United States departure from the Gold Exchange Standard. The "closing of the gold window" on August 15, 1971 and the measures that accompanied it was a policy package that has been sometimes praised, usually maligned, and almost always misunderstood. It has had consequences that were then unforeseeable, and that are now only beginning to unfold. Some believe that the mammoth hike in oil prices was triggered by the departure from gold.* Certainly currency gyrations and money terror have been among the consequences, with profound implications for the future of economies and societies throughout the world.

---

*"The oil crisis began a week after the dollar became formally inconvertible." Professor Robert Mundell, Columbia University in "The Santa Columba Conclusions—1976."

7

THE GUNS OF AUGUST

A billion dollars here, a billion dollars there . . . pretty soon it
begins to add up to real money.

EVERETT DIRKSON

"I never thought to see the day when a political leader could
make a triumph out of devaluation," growled Mr. John Kerby-
shire, a senior official of the Bank of England. It was Sunday
evening, December 18, 1971. President Nixon, an unblinking
grin congealed in TV makeup, was striding through the Great
Hall of the Smithsonian Institution at the head of a tight pack
of finance ministers and central bank chairmen from eleven
nations on his way to announce agreement for a new monetary
order that would "guarantee a generation of prosperity."

As it turned out, the Smithsonian Agreement, under which
the United States raised the price of gold by 8.3% and managed
to devalue the dollar against other currencies by amounts ranging from that same 8.3% to 17%, was but a colorful way-station
on the road to the collapse of the fixed-exchange-rate monetary
system and the onset of the modern world's first prolonged and
severe stagflation. How and when did we begin to take this
road?

Deterioration of the United States' trade and payments position in the 1960's was already generating concern over the via-
bility of the dollar as an effective and acceptable reserve currency for the rest of the world. However, the major turn

towards dollar disaster was taken late in that decade when the Administration of President Johnson attempted to finance the Great Society and the Viet Nam War without raising taxes. The alternative to higher taxes was to print money. In the years 1964–1967 the United States money supply (M1) grew at an average rate of 4.2% a year, peanuts in comparison with later splurges, but more than double the growth rate of the preceding four years. In 1968, money growth hit 7% and the fat was in the fire.

About this time we entered what might be called the "emperor's clothes" phase of the post-War Gold Exchange Standard. Theoretically, under the Gold Exchange Standard the central banks of other countries were permitted to turn in the dollars they had in their vaults for gold whenever they wished, and this was done with modest regularity during the 1950's and early 1960's. However, by 1968 it was apparent that we were running out of gold. United States gold reserves had declined to $10.9 billion from nearly $25 billion after the War. Dollars held by central banks of foreign countries and potentially convertible into gold already exceeded our gold supply. Thus, it was clear to our major overseas trading partners, Britain, France, Germany, and Japan, that any substantial request on their part for United States gold would have to be formally refused, an act which would effectively end the Gold Exchange Standard. The fiction of dollar convertibility was instead duly maintained by the device of greasing a few squeaky wheels. The Belgians, Dutch, and Swiss would periodically show up to exchange $30 to $50 million of the dollars held by their central banks for gold from Fort Knox. The United States would gracefully pay up, thereby proving that the world was still on a Gold Exchange Standard. Small countries stitched the emperor's clothes and were paid accordingly. This may sound childish in retrospect, but at the time, such things were done with great solemnity.

Meanwhile the dollar printing press at the Fed rolled on apace, if erratically. Up 7% in 1968, our money supply grew another 6% in 1969, 3.9% in 1970, and 6.7% in 1971. Such was the tempo of the times that the 1970 rate of "only" 3.9% was regarded as a "money squeeze."

However, during this period all eyes in Washington were

focused on a problem that seemed to have little to do with the creation of excess dollars in the United States. This problem was American trade. In 1964 our exports had exceeded our imports by a comfortable surplus of $6.8 billion. By 1969 this surplus had shrunk to $600 million, and worse was in store. To official Washington the reason was plain: our allies and trading partners were undercutting us in world markets and flooding the United States with cheap imports. A particular villain was Japan, already known as "Japan, Inc." whose disciplined society could turn out immense quantities of automobiles and electronic components and sell them for a song throughout the world and especially in the United States.

Even Canada, hardly a low wage economy, was running large trade surpluses with the United States. Canadian statistics differed substantially from our own regarding just how large this surplus was. One day in 1972, at a meeting with Canadian Finance Minister Edgar Benson, Treasury Secretary John Connally thundered forth about our trade deficit with Canada of "two BILLION dollars!" "What two billion dollars?" asked Benson, "It's only 1.2 billion dollars." To avert a crisis, the writer, present at the meeting, confessed that he had neglected to warn Connally that the Canadians had their own set of numbers. This is another example of the fallibility of the statistics upon which high economic policy is based. The American–Canadian border is traversed daily by thousands of trucks, each with its cargo of exports–imports. Customs officials do not usually clock the exports; counting of imports depends upon training, vigilance, and the time of day or night, all of which leaves the statistical raw material a bit shaky. A joint American-Canadian Commission was forthwith named to reconcile the sovereign statistics of both nations. Should such a reconciliation have been achieved by now, it would be a unique example of bureaucratic compromise. After the episode with Finance Minister Benson, Secretary Connally patriotically insisted that only American statistics be mentioned in any discussions with him.

Finally, there was the European Common Market, whose protectionist agricultural policy seemed deliberately designed to exacerbate the American trade problem—and alienate the farm vote.

At the root of these problems with our trading partners lay an additional and most intractible assymetry of the Gold Exchange Standard that must now be described in order to round out the picture of the post-War monetary system. The dollar was not only the currency in which most other countries kept their reserves and the currency in which most international transactions were denominated, the dollar was also the currency standard against which other countries set, or "pegged," the values of their own currencies. Pounds, marks, francs, lire, and yen were valued in practice not at so many grams of gold but at so and so many U.S. cents. Each country tried to value its currency at a rate that would bring a comfortable inflow of reserves and provide the maximum trade advantages. For these reasons, United States officials were convinced that it was impossible for the United States unilaterally to devalue the dollar. We could raise the dollar price of gold, but other currencies could and probably would remain pegged to the dollar at their old rates. A dollar would continue to equal 360 yen regardless of whether an ounce of gold were valued at $35 or $40.

This made for a sense of helpless frustration in Washington. Most of the official as well as academic thinking laid the blame for our trade problems on the "overvaluation" of the dollar, which meant the undervaluation of other currencies, but, with the exception of Germany and Switzerland, other nations were unwilling to revalue their own currencies, believing that such a step would hurt their exports and create domestic unemployment.

Meanwhile, a major change had occurred in American political alignments: organized labor, hitherto a staunch advocate of free trade, had turned protectionist and was backing a bill in Congress—the Burke-Hartke Bill—that would have sharply curtailed trade and investment abroad.

By the summer of 1971 the stage was set for disaster: the U.S. trade balance was worsening with no end in sight; the Administration was powerless to change the value of the dollar without the cooperation of other nations, a cooperation which had not been forthcoming and did not appear likely; and the domestic political balance had swung towards a protectionism capable of destroying the post-War trading system and plunging the world back into the beggar-thy-neighbor chaos of the

1930's. Against this background, speculation against the dollar in world money markets was growing apace. This meant that individuals and corporations who had dollars would sell them and buy marks, francs, yen, and even British pounds. The dollars thus sold landed up in the vaults of central banks as a theoretical claim against our gold. During 1970, foreign central bank holdings of dollars increased by $7.3 billion; in the first half of 1971 they rose again by $10.2 billion. On Friday, August 6, 1971, after a Congressional Committee declared its opinion that the dollar was overvalued, we lost another $1 billion; the following week we lost $3.7 billion. On Friday, the 13th, an official at the Bank of England was understood by an official at the Federal Reserve Bank of New York to have remarked, "I say, shouldn't you chaps be giving us a guarantee for all these dollars we're taking in?"

This remark was taken to mean that the Bank of England intended to ask for an exchange rate guarantee for the dollars they held, meaning that if the dollar were subsequently devalued—which is precisely what we hoped to accomplish—the Treasury Department, i.e., the American taxpayer, would have to cough up the difference. No official likes to face that prospect.

That Friday night the helicopter blades whirled, as top Treasury and other economic officials were air-lifted to Camp David in deepest secrecy. It has been noted that devaluations and major moves regarding money are invariably announced on the Sabbath. This was no exception. On Sunday, August 15, the United States Government announced that dollars henceforth would not be exchanged for gold for anybody, central bank or not. The Emperor was officially naked.

If the timing was traditional, the content of the August 15 policy announcement was original and highly controversial. For not only did we unilaterally terminate our obligation (by then largely theoretical) to honor claims on the dollar in gold, we also imposed a temporary 10% surcharge on all manufactured imports and slapped a freeze on domestic wages and prices.

The policy package had mixed reviews. Controversy centered around the 10% temporary surcharge, which brought cries of outrage from the traditionally internationalist Eastern Establishment and from many middle level officials in the State

The Emperor was officially naked

Department who hadn't even been consulted! It became known as the "Nixon Shock"—in Japanese, the "Nixon Shokku"—but the major animosity was focused on Treasury Secretary John Connally, who, as Administration Spokesman for Economic Policy, was widely, and correctly, perceived as its author. Critics were convinced that this high-handed move would forever destroy the trust of our allies.

However, if one looks at the policy package as a whole, against the background of events which precipitated it, a more charitable as well as more instructive view emerges. The central part of the package was the "closing of the gold window." It was the honest judgment of responsible and trained officials at the time that, because of the rush of speculation against the dollar, this step had to be taken and taken fast. Interestingly, American critics of *this* move have been relatively few. Once we had to close the gold window, the accompanying moves can be seen as both imaginative and politically necessary. Going off gold was an admission of defeat and good grounds for the epithet "paper tiger." Alone, it would have done nothing to improve the American trade position. Had it been the only step taken, our allies would have felt pity and condescension for the plight of a weak Uncle Sam, and would promptly have looked elsewhere for their future political and economic ties. Our own Congress would have returned from its summer recess loaded for bear in the form of emotional legislation to put world trade back into the 1930's.

The decision to add the 10% surcharge turned pity into rage overseas. Rage will pass, as it did in this case. Pity is indelible. The surcharge also defused a potential explosion in Congress. Since it was temporary, pending future negotiations about exchange rate changes with our trading partners, Congress agreed to wait upon these negotiations. Whatever has happened to the international monetary system since, there at least has been no major protectionist legislation in the United States. In a manner of speaking, the cause of free trade was saved by a measure that seemed to deny it.

Finally, the wage-price freeze served notice to the American public and to our aggrieved allies that we were taking steps to put our own house in order rather than simply slapping the faces of our trading partners. Whatever the ultimate merit of the wage-price freeze and subsequent Phase 1 and Phase 2 controls, they made us, for a time, the marvel of the Western World. Finance ministers from all over eagerly asked how on earth we managed to make them work.

Such is the anatomy of a policy, poorly understood and heavily criticized at the time—and largely forgotten in the rush of later events. The 10% surcharge ended with the conclusion of negotiations at the Smithsonian in December 1971. By agreement with our ten major trading partners, the United States symbolically devalued, by raising the dollar price of gold from $35 to $38 an ounce (symbolically, because no gold changed hands at either price) and the other countries revalued their currencies in varying amounts from 8.3% for the French franc to 17% for Japan's yen. (The Canadian dollar, which had been floating at the time, continued to float.) The negotiations to achieve this agreement resembled haggling in a Turkish bazaar, lending credence to earlier American fears that it would be most difficult to induce other countries to raise the values at which they pegged their currencies to the dollar. Indeed, without the lever of the temporary import surcharge, it is doubtful that any significant currency realignment could have been achieved.

Though President Nixon hailed the Smithsonian Agreement as the greatest monetary reform of all time, within 13 months the Smithsonian currency realignments proved insufficient to withstand market speculation. We devalued again, this time by ten percent; others revalued, but pretty soon the world was floating.

World money supply growth and inflation rates are three-quarter moving averages for Belgium, Canada, France, Germany, Italy, Japan, The Netherlands, The United Kingdom, The United States, and Switzerland. *(Courtesy:* Citibank Research Department.)

It is now time for a summary look at how the Great Inflation of the 1970's was engineered on a global scale. No nation escaped it. Most major price changes are worldwide in scope. The 1973 increase of 43% in American food prices was, for example, precipitated by a crop failure the preceding year in Soviet Russia. The four-fold oil price increase the following year was equally foreign in origin. But, above all, *money is a worldwide phenomenon.*

When the Fed conducted its first wave of money creation in the late 1960's to help President Johnson finance the Viet Nam War and Great Society, a large part of this money flowed abroad, Europe and Japan playing the reluctant Sparticas to our Illusia. The second wave started in 1970, when over $7 billion dollars landed up as high-powered reserves in the vaults of foreign central banks. The following year, 1971, this outflow rose to a climactic $27 billion. Foreign central banks had to accept these dollars whether they liked it or not, for the alternative was to let their currencies rise sharply in value, which would have done serious short-term damage to their export industries. The dollar reserves that they had to accept were "high powered" in the sense that they became in each country the monetary base for a pyramidal expansion of that country's money supply. The result was that when the United States money supply rose by 7% in 1971 the money supply of the Western World as a whole expanded by double that amount. The following chart illustrates how the upsurge in world money supply produced a world inflation.

To the worldwide implications of their actions the leadership of the Fed seemed blissfully oblivious. Concentrating sometimes on domestic interest rates, at other times on the domestic money supply, they helped to destroy first the Gold Exchange Standard and then the economic base of American political leadership, with nothing more than a bewildered glance at disquieting events overseas.

Not only were they unaware that massive increases in the world money supply could backfire on the United States through an explosion in world prices, they also studiously ignored a brand new phenomenon: the weed-like growth of a dollar banking system overseas. This system is called the Eurodollar Market.

Interestingly enough, Eurodollars were conceived during the Cold War 1950's by two banks that were owned and controlled by the Soviet Union: Narodny Bank in London and Banque du Nord et de l'Est in Paris. The Russians did not want to keep any dollars they had earned from exports or trading activities in American banks for fear that these dollars might be confiscated by the United States Government. To solve their problem, they hit on the idea of dollar balances in foreign-owned banks, starting with their own. The idea caught on widely after the Kennedy Administration introduced the Interest Equalization Tax and other measures in 1963 to slow down American investment overseas. Government regulations usually have unintended side-effects. (No government regulation has to be approved by a Food and Drug Administration that demands years of careful testing before something new is introduced.) The Interest Equalization Tax was no exception. Its side effect was a massive expansion of dollar lending by foreign banks, an activity into which foreign subsidiaries of American banks soon eagerly plunged. By 1970 Eurodollar deposits were close to $100 billion, by 1973, $200 billion, by 1976, $400 billion, and soon the figure will be $800 billion, dwarfing our domestic money supply (M1) of $370 billion.*

With its head firmly in the sand, the Fed elected to ignore this development, and sought academic justification for a policy of oblivion. In 1974, the Fed Board of Governors appointed an Advisory Committee on Monetary Statistics, chaired by Professor G. L. Bach of Stanford University, with five other distinguished professors, including Milton Friedman. This Committee duly made its report, which was published by the Fed in 1976. The report contained modest technical recommendations for modification of the various M's, but, when it came to Eurodollar deposits the Committee used a long broom and a large rug: "Given the theoretical difficulty of prescribing the 'ideal' inclusion of foreign—or international—money in the U.S. money stock, the practical difficulties of obtaining the desired data even if they could be conceptually defined, and the relatively small role played by international transactions in the

---

*According to estimates by Morgan Guaranty Trust Company. The Bank for International Settlements in Basle estimates Eurodollar deposits at about half these amounts.

U.S. economy, as a practical matter we recommend use of a concept of money focused primarily on the domestic economy." In translation, this reads: We don't know what kind of money Eurodollar deposits are: even if we did, we don't know how to measure them; they aren't very important anyway, so let's forget 'em.

The ability of this Committee to write, in mid-1976, that international transactions play a small role in the United States economy is an impressive demonstration of scholarship. It takes cloistered dedication to ignore a 100% increase in world food prices and a fourfold world oil price increase.

To this day there is disagreement among experts on the role that Eurodollars may or may not play in fueling U.S. and world inflation. This is but one more of the complexities of modern life with which economic theory has yet to cope.

After futile attempts to maintain some semblance of fixed exchange rates in 1972 and 1973, the major currencies of the world were floating by 1974. The divergent directions in which they floated had profoundly different impacts on price levels in each country. For example, from 1974 to the end of 1978, the German mark rose 54% against the U.S. dollar. American consumer prices rose 7.8% per annum over the same years, nearly double the 4.2% in Germany. In 1978 alone, when American prices lurched up 9%, German prices rose only 2.4%.

From all that has been said in the last three chapters, one would think that the Fed was printing money at double the rate of the German central bank. Strange to say, *the opposite was true.* The German money supply, as tabulated by the Federal Reserve Bank of St. Louis from German central bank figures, grew at 11.3% a year, nearly double the 6.1% of the United States. Allowing for the difficulties of comparing the money supplies of two different countries (such statistics for one country alone are dubious enough), the disparity is still striking. Given comparable growth rates in two countries, a much higher money supply increase in one should lead to *higher* rather than lower price increases and a *lower* exchange rate. What is missing?

What is missing is the final element in the story of money: the element of public psychology, or confidence. The Germans have the reputation of being unwilling to tolerate inflation.

Having lost their savings twice in a lifetime, in 1923 and after World War II, they will not support a government that offers a repeat performance. Rightly or wrongly, therefore, the German mark is seen as a safe haven, and in particular as a hedge against the deterioration of the dollar. By Arabs, by multinational corporations, and by gnomes in Zurich, German marks are collected—like postage stamps—as symbols of enduring value.

There is a lesson in this: management of paper money is an art, not a science. Like everything else in economics, it needs appreciation for human psychology. As long as credibility is maintained and the money is accepted as "sound," almost any amount of it can be printed. When credibility starts to disappear, the central bank had better pull in its horns before it is too late. History is littered with the demises of civilizations whose rulers continued to clip coins after their subjects had caught on to what they were doing.

Restoring to the dollar the public confidence it once enjoyed and which is now given to the German mark, the Swiss franc and the Japanese yen, will be the central challenge both for the United States economy and for world security in the next decade. Meeting this challenge will benefit both. At the same time there are other steps that the United States can take, in tax and regulatory policy, to strengthen itself.

8

LOOKING THROUGH
THE LOOPHOLE

If your brother commits a sin . . . and if he will not listen even to
the congregation, you must treat him as you would a pagan or a
tax gatherer."

MATTHEW
18:15–20

As prostitution is the oldest profession in the private sector, so
is the collection of taxes the oldest branch of civil service. From
earliest times there have been three distinct purposes of taxation: 1) financing government—the rulers, their bureaucrats,
and their armies; 2) redistributing wealth from those with less
to those with more political clout; 3) implementing public policy. The taxes levied by Pharoah upon the Children of Israel
served to support the Egyptian State, to redistribute wealth
from the nonvoting Israelite to Pharoah and his officials and, in
furtherance of public policy, to persecute the Jews. The followers of Moses responded by setting an important precedent.
Emigration, now called the "brain drain," is virtually the only
way to escape the tax collector.

These three functions of taxation remain with us in every
modern society, no matter how barbaric or civilized. Government and the military must be paid for. Income is regularly
redistributed by the tax system from the unorganized general
public to any group with enough voting clout to catch the ears
of lawmakers: the poor and the aged, of course, but also a wide
array of special groups, including farmers, teachers, civil ser-
vants, veterans, and municipal workers, plus the constituents of
any lawmaker who can secure a public works project in his or

her district. Finally, taxation has become a sophisticated tool of public policy—not just to persecute certain people or restrain certain activities, but sometimes to encourage efforts that might not otherwise be made. This is the purpose of the tax loophole.

The systematic use of tax loopholes is a relatively modern phenomenon, because the tax loophole is not effective without high tax rates. The tax to be avoided must be severe, otherwise the loophole will not be attractive enough to entice people to walk through it. High tax rates arrived in the United States after passage of the Sixteenth Amendment, allowing for the progressive income tax, in 1913.

Each loophole on our tax books originally had a purpose, and many still do. Oil depletion allowances were specifically designed to encourage discovery and extraction of petroleum. Tax-free municipal bonds were, and are, a means of reducing borrowing costs to states and municipalities. Deduction of mortgage payments encourages housing construction. And so on down through a large list of understandings by which Congress has said to the taxpayer: "If you will put your money or effort into such and such an area, we will lower your taxes."

It has already been pointed out in earlier chapters what a hit-or-miss proposition most government economic policy is apt to be. By contrast, tax loopholes can be a remarkably accurate policy rifle, provided it is understood that their purpose is to get something done rather than to reward the one who is doing it. There is, of course, every reason to reexamine each existing loophole regularly and rigorously. But, when loopholes are judged, the criterion should be whether the tax-favored activity, such as drilling for oil, is still in the national interest, and not who benefits from it.

Presidential candidates habitually pledge to eliminate all tax loopholes. The appeal is simple and demagogic: thanks to these loopholes, some people manage to reduce their tax bills, which is unfair to the rest. Forgotten is the fact that these same people, were it not for the tax loophole, would be investing their money and effort in other more profitable areas and neglecting those which Congress apparently thought desirable for the nation. Most of our politicians prefer to concentrate, not on the merits of the loopholes themselves, but on the evil of the people who have been deliberately induced to use them. If all loopholes were eliminated, a small number of people would land up paying higher taxes, but Government would have lost its best policy tool.

Closely allied to the demagogy about loopholes is the most fraudulent free lunch of them all: taxing "big business." Nearly all politicians, including many conservatives who are defensive about it, believe that in our corporations there is a great store of wealth which can be tapped, either to lower individual taxes or to finance antipoverty programs. Regrettably, this is simply not true. Corporations do not bleed and cannot be bled. Only people bleed, and the only way to transfer income or wealth from the rich to the poor is to tax rich *people* and turn the proceeds over to poor *people*. When corporations are heavily taxed it is people who get hit and very often precisely those people who can least afford it.

A little simple arithmetic will make this point clear. Suppose Consolidated Construction Corp. is earning $20 million, before taxes, on sales of $100 million. The corporate income tax is 50% or $10 million, leaving $10 million of after tax profit for Consolidated. Of this $10 million, $5 million is paid in dividends to the stockholders and $5 million is reinvested in the business. If the corporate income tax rate is raised to 75%, or $15 million, Consolidated will be left with only $5 million, forcing a cutback of either dividends or expansion or both. However, in all likelihood, Consolidated will try to raise prices in order to maintain its former after tax income. On the same physical output and with the same costs, a price rise of 20% to $120 million would produce a pretax income of $40 million, of which the Treasury would get $30 million—$20 million more than before the tax increase—and Consolidated would get $10 million—the same as before. Thus, if the response to a corporate income tax increase is to raise prices, the effect becomes the same as a sales tax on Consolidated's products. The consumer pays. A sales tax would have been more honest, but would be hotly opposed by the same labor union leaders who ardently advocated the corporate income tax increase.

Of course, instead of raising prices, Consolidated could eliminate the $5 million of spending for expansion. This would mean no growth in production and no growth in employment. If the demand for Consolidated's products continued to rise, however, prices would eventually rise to the point where Consolidated could generate enough money to resume its expansion. Thus far, the only ones hit by this increase in taxes on "big business" are consumers and, indirectly, employees.

If, on the other hand, Consolidated decided to eliminate its dividend, the shareholders would be hurt, and the government would lose the personal income tax revenues which it had been garnering from their dividends. This would cause the shareholders to sell their stock leaving Consolidated unable to finance any expansion through the capital markets. Business expansion in a capitalist country is financed through a mixture of internally generated funds, debt, and new equity money from shareholders. Tampering, through taxation, with any of these sources of funds is bound to have an impact on expansion.

Thus, the corporate income tax is paid, not by the corporation, which has no blood to give, but by its customers, its workers, or its shareholders, many of them pension funds. The net effect of increasing the corporate income tax is apt to be increased prices and increased unemployment. In economists' jargon, the corporate income tax is "regressive," that is, it is paid by those least able to pay. Certainly there is one group of people whom the corporate income tax does not hit: the people who run the corporations. Executive salaries are paid out of pretax income, and the higher the corporate tax rate the lower is the after tax cost of the president's salary.

Returning to our original example of Consolidated Construction, suppose the corporate income tax is *reduced* from 50% to 25%. At a tax rate of 50%, Consolidated had $10 million after taxes for expansion and dividends. Now, thanks to a conservative Congress, Consolidated has $15 million. If Consolidated elects to pay the additional $5 million out in dividends, the deliriously happy shareholders (except for tax-free pension funds) will find themselves paying personal income taxes to the government on their increased dividends at marginal rates up to 70%, which is not a bad deal for the Treasury. If Consolidated decides to reinvest its extra $5 million in plant and equipment, employment will rise, incidentally boosting tax revenues, and, as more output comes on the market, prices will fall.

But, don't these giant corporations secrete a store of wealth somewhere, wealth that can be tapped for the man in the street, so that his income taxes can be lowered? The answer is no—not unless the corporation is badly managed. Any available wealth is used as expeditiously as possible to create more wealth, which can only come from more products or new products, and, with that, new jobs. If the corporation is badly managed, it will eventually be taken over by someone who can manage it properly, unless, like Amtrac, it is already owned by the government.

Sad as it is to report, and hard as it may be to believe, corporate income taxes do not redistribute income. Quite the contrary, they hit the little fellow, inhibit expansion, and discourage employment. However, they can have a purpose: corporate taxes allow the government to exert a direct influence on the economy—through loopholes. A notable example of this kind of manipulation is the investment tax credit. First proposed by the Kennedy Administration, the investment tax credit offers a reduction in corporate taxes if the corporation invests in plant and equipment. Here was the deliberate use of a tax loophole to achieve a specific national purpose: the expansion of productive capacity. The policy seems to have worked. Although one can never know what would have happened in the absence of this particular tax concession, the 1960's, after its enactment, were years of sustained and rapid growth. This loophole is still on the books.

A more sophisticated example is to be found in Sweden, a "socialist" country that occasionally demonstrates a capitalist mentality. There the corporate income tax is postponed on those profits which a company is willing to deposit in an account with the central bank. This money can be used tax-free, but only for plant expansion, and then only when the Swedish government decides that there is a cyclical downturn which warrants the stimulus of capital expenditure. Then the government says, "Go!" The corporations spend their tax-free money and the economy gets a shot in the arm. Ironically to an American, it often has been the Swedish trade unions that have agitated for tax-free release of these corporate funds at the first signs of a cyclical downturn.

The potential for using tax loopholes to carry out government policy has hardly been realized. People will do almost

anything to avoid death or taxes. If corporations are given
credit on their tax bills for putting in a new machine, why not
give employers as much or more credit for hiring more labor?
The possible benefits of an employment tax credit are discussed
in detail in a later chapter.

Turning now to the subject of individual taxes, as against
corporate taxes, there is a fundamental truism, recently discovered by *avant-garde* economists: if the tax rate is 100%, tax
receipts will be zero, because nobody will work full time for the
tax collector. The relationship between the tax *rate* and the tax
revenue, actually realized by the Treasury, is shown by the following diagram, based on the assumptions that at a rate of zero
percent, tax revenues will be zero, and that at a rate of 100%,
tax revenues will also be zero.

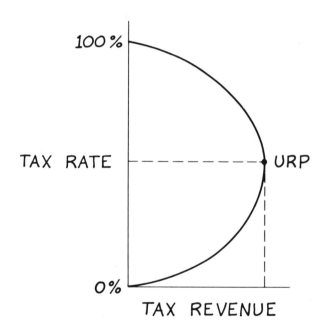

This simple concept has been recently popularized as the "Laffer
Curve," named for its unveiler, Professor Arthur Laffer. Under
this concept, the goal of tax rate-setting is to hit the ultimate
revenue point (URP) which is that rate at which the citizenry can
be milked to the maximum.

The Laffer Curve has aroused intense controversy. Some
critics fly in the face of logic to maintain that it doesn't exist.

The U.S. Treasury Department and foreign finance ministries, in particular, habitually calculate that any tax increase will produce proportionally more revenue, because they assume that people will work just as long and hard after a tax increase as before. By this reasoning, a 100% tax rate will produce the maximum revenue! Many people automatically accept these Treasury and finance ministry calculations simply because they are printed on government stationery.

However, in the real world, when tax rates are raised past a certain point, people either work less or they resort to barter. An example of the latter would be the fortuitous meeting of a doctor and a lawyer, both in high tax brackets. The doctor needs a divorce and the lawyer an operation. They exchange their services, with no payment on either side, and the only loser is the Treasury.

Other critics maintain, with some justification, that the Laffer Curve is fine in theory, but that in practice we do not know either the shape of the curve or where our tax rates presently ride upon it. The left, or high URP curve is typical of a well-disciplined society, in particular a nation at war, when citizens are willing to work almost regardless of financial reward. After the war is over, the Laffer Curve is apt to droop towards a low-URP configuration, as shown on the right. Maintaining high wartime tax rates after the war is over can not only kill economic growth, it can reduce tax revenues way below their

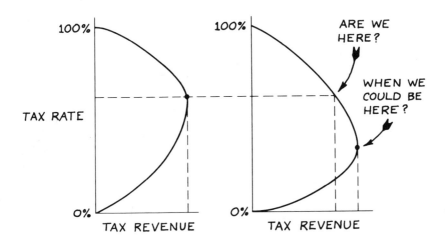

potential. This is what the British did with disastrous consequences after World War I and World War II. By contrast,
the United States reduced tax rates sharply in 1921, and in
successive years thereafter, fueling the boom of the 1920's.
American tax rates were also lowered after the Second World
War, though not so sharply. Germany and Japan remained in
the high tax doldrums until 1948 (for Germany) and 1950 (for
Japan), when authorities initiated policies of tax reduction
which were largely responsible for the German and Japanese
"economic miracles."

These points and more are brought out in a carefully
documented study by Jude Wanniski.* Items:

The stock market crash of 1929 coincided with debate on and
  ultimate passage of the Smoot Hawley tariff act.

Herbert Hoover increased the income tax in 1932, guaran-
  teeing the depression.

Roosevelt raised taxes in 1935 and again in 1936, producing
  the depression-within-a-depression of 1937.

Kennedy proposed a tax rate cut, signed by Johnson, which
  brought the stock market from 600 to 1,100 in three years
  and led to a period of rapid growth in the economy.

Nixon's 1969 "Tax Reform Act," which closed "loopholes"
  was followed by the doldrums of the 1970's.

Wanniski's—and Laffer's—point seems to be that nations in
the modern world tend to set their tax rates somewhere *above*
the URP of. maximum revenue. Therefore, at any given moment in history a lowering of tax rates will produce greater
economic activity and a higher tax take. Here is where the
critics zero in. They say that we might be *below* the ultimate
revenue point, in which case we cannot afford the risk of a tax
cut that would diminish tax revenues. Liberals worry about
reduced opportunities for government spending; conservatives
worry about a larger budget deficit. Moralists worry that any
reduction in the rate of taxes being paid by rich people will

---

*Jude Wanniski, *The Way the World Works*, Basic Books, 1978.

undermine the social fabric, creating vaster gulfs between rich and poor.

These objections, however irrational and emotional their origins, must be answered, if the public and its representatives are to be persuaded that lower tax rates can produce both prosperity and equity. To do so, the Laffer Curve must be broken into its component parts.

9

MAXIMUM REVENUE, MINIMUM PAIN

The challenge of tax policy is to devise a structure of rates that will promote an active and successful economy, but will at the same time satisfy popular demand for fairness. To many people, "fairness" means, in the elegant words of a *New York Times* editorial,[1] that the "rich" should be "soaked." Even if one accepts for a moment this crude concept of economic justice, it is necessary first to identify the "rich" before the soaking process takes place. No one wants to soak the poor by mistake.

In the last chapter, it was pointed out that industrial corporations are not rich in the same sense that some people are rich. A corporation may have vast sums of money to its name, but these sums are used to carry out and to expand its business. If the money is taxed away, then the corporation must charge higher prices, or cease expanding, or even go out of business. This unavoidable fact explains much of the economic trouble that the United States is currently suffering. It will come as a surprise to most Americans that corporate taxes have increased alarmingly during the past decade as a result of inflation. This may sound strange, because the corporate tax rate has remained somewhat below 50% of profits through the decade. The problem has been that the profits of a business are what is left over after expenses, including the cost of materials, labor, and equipment. Material and labor costs rise, of course, with inflation, but the cost of equipment is another matter. Equipment wears out and must be replaced. Recognizing this, the tax laws allow a company to put aside money each year—called depreciation—for this eventual replacement. However, the tax laws do not as yet recognize that in a decade of inflation the cost of replacing this equipment may double. Because of this little oversight in the tax code, it is possible for a corporation, unlike an individual, to pay taxes at over 100% of its profits.

Here's how this happens. Returning to Consolidated Construction: it had sales of $100 million and made a profit of $20 million, on which it paid taxes of $10 million. It also had factories and machines with an original cost of $110 million and a useful life of 10 years. Under the tax laws Consolidated was allowed to set aside $11 million a year in depreciation to pay for the eventual purchase of new plants and machines. However, the rate of inflation was such that prices would double, making the replacement cost $220 million at the end of the decade. A prudent president of Consolidated would earmark $2 million each year to replace his equipment before considering that he had any profits whatsoever. After allowing the extra $11 million toward replacement costs, Consolidated's real earnings were only $9 million before taxes. But, the Internal Revenue Service allows neither prudence nor reality for tax purposes. Consolidated's tax, therefore, remained at $10 million, 111% of the $9 million profit. After a decade of this, Consolidated went out of business.

This deliberately simplified example is designed to convey today's reality for many companies in many businesses. According to a study made in 1977, if the aftertax earnings of Alcoa, Bethlehem Steel, Goodyear, and International Harvester were properly stated by allowing for inflation's impact on the cost of replacing assets, their earnings would be negative.[2] In other words, these companies were paying over 100% in taxes. If an individual's income tax rate reached 100%, he or she would simply stop working or turn to barter. A corporation has no such choice. It goes on functioning while its machinery gets older and older. Then, one after another, plants are closed and workers laid off. Politicians lay the blame on import competition and poor corporate management. Corporate executives can only plod on, pleading sometimes for relief from the crushing tax burden and collecting, always, their salaries. The people who get hurt are workers, consumers, and shareholders, many of the latter being pension funds upon which workers must depend for their retirement.

The philosophy behind business taxation in America is a prime example of shooting at the wrong target. Nobody who is rich is soaked by taxing "big business," but the man in the street is bled heavily. At the same time, the nation's capacity for regeneration is strangled. One thing to be said for a socialist planned economy in the Soviet style is that such blundering in the broad allocation of resources would be unthinkable even in Moscow. Planners decide what proportion of total national output should go into investment without the ideological worry that the investment they plan might make somebody rich.

Who, then, is rich—and soakable? There is a great confusion about this in the public mind. It is the confusion between income and wealth. When Barbara Walters earns a million dollars a year, she is considered to be "rich," with a richness worthy of newspaper attention. Teddy Kennedy is also "rich," but the statistics of his wealth do not make news. There is a profound difference between these two types of richness, but the difference is usually ignored. No matter what she does, short of the right marriage, Barbara Walters can never accumulate anything like the fortune built up by Teddy Kennedy's father. This was a gain gotten before the income tax reached its present proportions. It is *wealth,* not *income.*

Despite this difference between wealth and income and despite the existence of 500,000 millionaires in this country, the Great Tax Debate revolves almost exclusively around *income* taxes. Conservatives argue, in line with the Laffer Curve, that lower tax rates in upper income brackets are necessary to provide adequate incentive, to stimulate the economy, and to increase tax revenue. Liberals argue that high income tax rates will produce equally high tax revenues and, more important, will narrow the gulf between rich and poor. Great wealth slides stealthily by.

What is wealth? Regardless of orders of magnitude, wealth is the same as savings, capital, or assets. A wage earner whose income is $20,000 and who has $12,000 in the bank can regard the $12,000 as his or her wealth. Under the tax laws he or she will have a hard time increasing that nest egg. A legislator who makes $55,000 in salary but who has a family fortune of $50 million can regard that $50 million with all its power as his wealth.

Income in the United States is taxed, and taxed at heavily increasing rates. Wealth is also taxed, but it is taxed in a capricious fashion. There are three distinct wealth taxes. The first is inflation—a concealed tax which hits primarily small savers who cannot afford to hedge their wealth in real estate, commodities, or gold. Their money is in the bank or, trustingly, in government bonds. Inflation's wealth tax upon the not-so-wealthy is by now well over 10% a year.

The second wealth tax is the inheritance tax—a macabre piece of legislation dreamt up not only to produce revenue but to promote "fairness." The advent of death in a family, not normally the happiest of events, is rendered more lugubrious by the presence of a Government Ghoul, the tax collector, who takes this solemn occasion to slice a substantial part away from the family wealth.

The third and least rational wealth tax is the tax on capital gains. This tax is levied when any person moves his or her savings from one asset to another with a view to investing the savings as sensibly as possible. If one investment has been successful, then changing it into another requires paying a substantial—up to 28%—tax to the government.

In the first chapter of this book, it was pointed out that the essential objective of economic policy—be it communist, socialist, or capitalist—is to allocate resources as quickly and efficiently as possible. A tax which deliberately prevents the smooth movement of people's savings out of less attractive investments and into more attractive ones thwarts the achievement of this objective. Imagine a Soviet Government planner being told that his salary would be docked if he advocated moving resources from steel production to computer research! The private investor, whose function is to allocate resources in a capitalist economy, is being told precisely that. If investors wish to move their money from U.S. Steel to IBM, they must pay a tax on any gain they made in U.S. Steel and prepare to pay a tax on any gain they might make in IBM.

Most of the argument over the capital gains tax—on the part of those who want to reduce it as well as from those who want to increase it—has missed this essential point: the capital gains tax is a wealth tax—most particularly a tax on resource reallocation—not an income tax. Public and politicians alike have an image of somebody who *makes money* by gambling in stocks, real estate, commodities, or whatever. Some people may indeed be able to augment their wealth in such a fashion. Most won't. But, whether or not somebody is wise or lucky should not blind us to the essential point that shifting assets from one investment to another is not the same as earning taxable income.

When the progressive income tax was introduced with the Sixteenth Amendment in 1913, capital gains were somehow included in the concept of income. A practical, if not theoretical, distinction between capital gains and income was recognized in 1921, when the tax rate on capital gains was reduced to half of the rate on income. Unhappily, the logical distinction between the two was never appreciated, so that to this day President Carter and many others genuinely believe that capital gains are the same as income, and therefore, that any reduced rate of taxation on capital gains is a "loophole."

Together with President Carter, those opposed to lowering the capital gains tax—widening the loophole—include both the AFL-CIO and the Business Roundtable, an organization that represents some 190 major corporations.[3] This strange bedfellowship is not so surprising as one would imagine. A high capital gains tax poses an enormous barrier to the movement of capital from mature established businesses into young, struggling, and risky enterprises. Thus it creates captive shareholders for old-line industry. Because the price of moving out is high, captive capitalists are created who continue to support mature—and usually unionized—corporations long after a rational market judgment would have made them move their money elsewhere. Such a tax policy wreaks incalculable damage to the United States economy by blocking the flow of money into areas of new technology, higher productivity, and human innovation.

In order to appreciate this, one need only look at recent history. The maximum tax rate on capital gains was raised by

President Nixon in 1969 from 25% to 49%. As a result, new stock issues of small, aspiring businesses—the IBM's and Xerox's of the future—fell from several hundred per year in the 1960's to exactly four in 1975. In 1978, Congress reduced capital gains taxes somewhat with the result that the supply of "venture capital"—the savings of people who are willing to take risks—snapped back.

In addition to choking off the flow of capital into growth industries, high tax rates on capital gains unquestionably produce low revenues. The capital gains tax is an extreme example of a sagging Laffer Curve. When the Nixon Administration raised this tax, the Treasury Department estimated—on the typical Treasury assumption of unchanged public behavior despite a tax increase—that this "reform" would add $1.1 billion to revenues in 1970 and $3.2 billion annually by 1975. Instead, revenues from the capital gains tax fell sharply.

The fact that the capital gains tax is not an income tax explains why the Laffer Curve sags so sadly. If the tax collector is reasonably efficient—and our IRS certainly is—then people have little choice but to pay their income taxes. Only when tax rates are very high, do people stop working. The capital gains

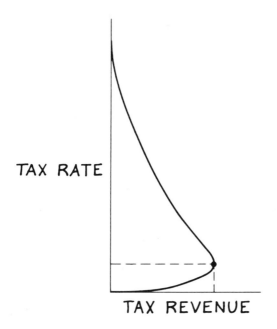

TAX RATE

TAX REVENUE

tax, however, is levied on transactions that are in most cases optional. People usually do not *have* to sell their houses, their paintings, or their stocks. They may wish to sell, but if the government makes the cost of selling prohibitive, then they stay with what they have and the government loses the potential tax revenue. This elementary logic is borne out by statistical evidence. A study prepared in 1978 under the auspices of the National Bureau of Economic Research indicated that "estimates of tax revenue change resulting from a reduction in capital gains taxation based on the assumption of unchanged realized gains may be misleading.[4] After the capital gains tax increase of 1969, realized gains from the sale of capital assets dropped by 34%, and, adjusting for inflation, never recovered to prereform levels. An argument might be made that the stock market since 1969 has not been conducive to the realization of large capital gains, but then one is faced with the question: which was cause and which effect? Did the increase in capital gains taxes cause the stock market to behave badly, or did poor stock market performance result in reduced capital gains revenues? When the National Bureau has enough data to study the effects of 1978's modest decrease in capital gains taxes, that question may be answered.

Parenthetically, the capital gains tax may turn into precisely the policy tool that has been needed for a long time. If past is guide to future, then we will sometime again be in a situation, like 1929 or 1968, when the nation's economic boom has gone so far as to worry the authorities. At such times in the past, it has fallen to the Federal Reserve to attempt to curb the boom. Former Federal Reserve chairman William McChesney Martin referred to this duty as "taking the punch bowl away in the middle of the party." John Kenneth Galbraith, in his account of the 1929 Crash, likened the task to that of deflating a bubble: "A bubble can be easily punctured. But to incise it with a needle so that it subsides gradually is a task of no small delicacy."[5] The capital gains tax may be just such a needle. If, during times when speculative fever is running amok, the government raises the capital gains tax on all securities purchased thereafter, people would be forced to think twice before engaging in further speculation, and the bubble could be gently deflated. Conversely, during periods of pessimism, the capital gains tax could be lowered to encourage the few far-seeing optimists to take a chance. In this manner the capital gains tax could be turned into a flexible tool for curbing the excesses of speculation during a boom and for nurturing the embers of optimism during a bust.

However, neither common sense nor statistical evidence will persuade those whose conviction it is that the primary purpose of taxation is not to raise revenue, not to improve the economy, not even to help the poor, but rather to "soak the rich." There is some irony in this viewpoint, for the capital gains tax tends to soak those who are attempting to get rich rather than those who already are. The truly rich are the ones who are least likely to be forced to sell assets upon which they would then have to pay capital gains. The truly rich are those who have already made their capital gains. And the liberal rich would rather raise than lower the capital gains tax—always in the name of "fairness."

The controversy over the capital gains tax highlights the recurring dilemma of tax policy in a democratic country: how to preserve incentive and efficiency while at the same time convincing the broad public that the system is fair. How can the Ultimate Revenue Point on the Laffer Curve be effectively milked without the appearance of favoring the rich? The answer, I think, is a direct wealth tax, levied on financial and nonfarm real estate assets above a certain net worth figure. Based on Internal Revenue Service estimates of personal wealth in America, one can roughly calculate that a wealth tax of one percent per annum, levied on personal net worth in excess of $200,000, would provide between $10 and $20 billion of revenues to the Treasury. The increase in taxes received from this particular soaking should calm the objections of budget balancers long enough to allow for an experiment with reduction of the capital gains tax. Such a reduction to, say, 10%, would *increase* capital gains tax revenues. In this fashion the rich and not-yet-rich would each find themselves contributing mightily to overall tax revenues. The rich might complain, but the not-yet-rich would enjoy the change. The public at large would have the feeling that wealthy families were at least in some degree being taxed.

In all fairness to families who have accumulated some degree of wealth, the annual tax paid on this wealth should be counted as a credit against inheritance taxes—a "pay as (or rather before) you go" formula akin to witholding taxes. In this way, medium rich families would be less cruelly deprived of their assets upon the death of the breadwinner, and small businesses would be made less subject to distress sales to pay inheritance taxes.

An honest, direct wealth tax would answer the political imperative of reducing the apparent gulf between rich and poor, while avoiding the conundrum of the Laffer Curve. For, it cannot be argued that a wealth tax would reduce the incentive to *earn* money. Quite to the contrary, a wealth tax would increase the incentive for the rich to work and take risks in order to preserve what they already have. More scions of wealthy families might choose to enter business rather than politics.

The idea of a wealth tax is likely to be unpopular in many circles that count. Wealthy liberals, whose concept of fairness is the absence of competition at the top of the economic and social ladder, will take a dim view of it, a view well-enough financed to carry weight. As for rich conservatives, whose wealth is more often self-made and therefore highly prized, a new encroachment will be viewed as threatening. If the proposal for a wealth tax is combined with reduction in income and capital gains taxes, however, conservatives should appreciate the competitive challenge. Those who have made their wealth themselves usually don't mind making an effort to preserve it.

Even if a wealth tax might appear doomed initially, the very act of proposing it for public debate will serve to clear away some intellectual and moral cobwebs. How many of those, already rich, who advocate highly progressive income and capital gains taxes levied on those who must work in order to pay for welfare, medical care, and government jobs, will maintain this enthusiasm when their own oxen are gored?

Of course, there are solid arguments against a wealth tax. Because this tax would prove to be a successful way of raising revenue, it could easily be abused. Would the political camel, having put its nose in the tent, stop there? One answer is that wealth is already being taxed—on a hit-or-miss basis—by inflation, inheritance taxes, and the capital gains tax. A direct, uniform tax would be better for almost all concerned. Another point is that some foreign countries have had wealth taxes—

Germany at 0.5%, Holland at 0.8%, Switzerland at varying levels depending upon the canton—for nearly a century without abusing them. However, the major reason for risking the introduction of a wealth tax is that it is probably the only way to achieve a reduction in other taxes that are crippling the economy in the name of fairness.

"Fairness" can be viewed either as equalization of incomes at the bottom with a quiet class entrenchment at the top, or as the preservation of hope: that anyone who tries hard enough and who has enough luck can move from bottom to top. The Established Person—politician, labor leader, academic intellectual, or simple scion of wealth—often prefers to see fairness as an equality of subjugation for everybody else, their needs taken care of and their aspirations successfully dulled.

The purpose of these chapters on taxation has not been to outline a complete ideal tax structure. There can be no such thing, for taxes are inherently unfair, and all taxes, to a greater or lesser degree, undermine incentives. Rather, it has been to make the point that some of our present taxes do unnecessary damage to the economy, hit the wrong targets and/or collect less revenue at present rates than at lower ones.

1. Corporate taxes are paid primarily by workers and consumers. They are not paid by corporate officers, and most of the shareholders who get nicked are the beneficiaries of pension funds. Far from a device to take from the rich and give to the poor, the corporate profits tax is closer to a concealed sales tax, easy to collect, and paid without protest by an unsuspecting public. The effective increase in this tax due to inflation is literally stifling the American economy.
2. Lowering the upper rates of personal income taxes will probably increase rather than lower actual tax revenues. It deserves to be tried.
3. Sharply lower capital gains taxes would almost certainly produce higher tax revenues, while promoting more rapid and rational allocation of investment resources.
4. Because most of the American people, however mistakenly, would regard any reduction in corporate, capital gains, and high bracket income tax rates as unfairly favoring the rich, a direct wealth tax might be a suitable answer. Such a tax

would finally assure the public that no team of accountants and lawyers could enable a person to escape taxes entirely.

The purpose of any tax changes should be to join the opportunity and incentive for upward mobility with proper, compassionate care for those who remain at the bottom of the economic ladder. It should also be to seek the URP of maximum tax revenue.

10
UNEMPLOYMENT

Traditionally the most emotionally charged economic issue in American politics, or for that matter the politics of any nation, is unemployment. This is understandable, for nothing is so cruel to the individual or disruptive to the social fabric than prolonged unemployment. Fortunately, in modern times unemployment is usually not as large as the statistics say it is.

The conventional picture of somebody unemployed is that of a worker who has lost a job and is rather desperately looking for another one. Yet, in May 1975, at the low point of that year's recession, when the official unemployment rate was 9%, *only 4% were looking for work as their major activity*. Most of the rest were keeping house, going to school, or more or less retired. This startling statistic comes from a paper on the Nature and Measure of Unemployment prepared at the National Bureau of Economic Research.[1]

Nonetheless adult unemployment becomes a serious matter at each ebb of the business cycle, while youth unemployment is a permanent problem of long-range significance. How has our government tried to combat unemployment over the years? What has it done inadvertently to create unemployment? What, if anything, can it do to alleviate the problem?

The major weapon thus far employed by the American Gov-

ernment in the battle against unemployment has been incantation. From the Employment Act of 1946 through the Full Employment and Balanced Growth Act of 1976 to the Hum-
phrey–Hawkins Bill of 1978, Congress has delivered regular
legislative incantations against unemployment. No party plat-
form or political campaign has been without its ritual exorcism
of the unemployment devil. The effectiveness of all this voodoo
is difficult to evaluate with existing tools of economic analysis.

At least incantation is harmless. The same cannot be said of
government efforts to fight unemployment using the broad
brush of fiscal and monetary policy. These efforts have tended
to produce inflation, so much so, that the necessity of enduring
inflation in order to reduce unemployment has become embedded in the public mind. Conversely, most people accept the
notion that the only way to fight inflation is to increase unemployment. If the phrase "the poor have been made cannon
fodder in the war against inflation" has not yet been seen or
heard in the media, it probably will be before long.

For economists, the idea of a "trade-off" between unemployment and inflation has been immortalized in the Phillips
Curve, named for its inventor, the late Professor A. W. Phillips
of the London School of Economics and the Australian National University. The Phillips Curve attempts to depict how
much unemployment a nation will have to endure at each level
of the inflation rate, and how much inflation at each level of
unemployment. On a graph it looks like a new moon sailing
North-East, because in recent years we have been experiencing
more inflation and *more* unemployment at the same time.

Attitudes and policies based upon a belief in this Phillips
Curve tend either to condemn a helpless minority to unemployment as the price of price stability or to condemn the vast
majority to intolerable inflation as the price of compassion for
the unemployed. This pits social groups against one another.
Minorities view askance any attempts to control inflation as
being liable to increase their own levels of unemployment.
Others view government efforts to reduce unemployment as a
threat to the value of their incomes and savings.

The idea embodied in the Phillips Curve is not only socially
destructive, it is analytically simplistic in the extreme. This is

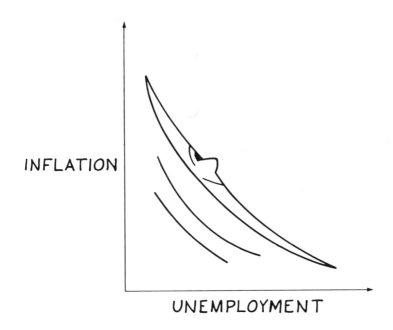

largely due to the fact that unemployment itself is usually thought of as a homogeneous phenomenon, whereas in reality it is an extremely complex problem with many manifestations and just as many causes. The balance of this chapter will take up the major kinds of unemployment (often overlapping) and their respective causes in the following order:

Frictional Unemployment

Cyclical Unemployment

Voluntary Temporary Unemployment

Permanent Unemployment (voluntary and involuntary)

Youth Unemployment.

FRICTIONAL UNEMPLOYMENT

Frictional unemployment stems from job changing in a mobile society. Much of this is voluntary, and even if involuntary, it is probably not unhealthy. Because of the inevitable nature of frictional unemployment, a 4% unemployment rate has usually been accepted as tantamount to "full employment." In recent years, frictional unemployment has risen somewhat due to the increased numbers of women and students in the labor force. Both tend to move more frequently into and out of the labor force as they seek jobs and later return to their respective hearths and studies. In the Nixon–Ford years, the President's Council of Economic Advisors raised this quaintly termed "full employment unemployment" rate to 5%, but drafters of the Humphrey-Hawkins Bill resolutely put it back down at 4%.

CYCLICAL UNEMPLOYMENT

Cyclical unemployment results from layoffs due to recessions. It is the one and only kind of unemployment that can be treated by attempts to end the recessions themselves. The closest available measure of cyclical unemployment is the unemployment rate among adult male heads of households. As Peter F. Drucker points out, this is what was meant by unemployment during the Great Depression because the work force was largely made up of adult male heads of households, and when they were thrown out of work, the hardship was acute.[2] With changing life-styles and especially the larger number of working women, this criterion for measuring cyclical unemployment may have become somewhat blurred, but it is still useful for distinguishing recession-caused unemployment from other types.

There is little indication in recent years that inflation has done much to stem cyclical unemployment or *vice versa*. Over the past seven years, this rate has ranged from 2% to over 6% at the low point of the 1975 recession. However, inflation has averaged about 8% a year. By contrast, if we take a nostalgic look at the Eisenhower, Kennedy, and early Johnson years, 1952–67, when government policy was less activist, the unemployment rate for these male household heads fluctuated between 1.5% and 5%, but only in one year, 1966, did the rate of inflation rise fractionally above 3%. This suggests that cyclical full employment has not been the villain behind our inflation, and also that a rise in unemployment is unlikely to bring down inflation.

Nonetheless, cyclical unemployment will always rise during

recessions. What can be done to tackle this problem? A possible approach to reducing cyclical unemployment without risking inflation received some public and congressional attention following the 1975 recession. This approach calls for substantial temporary tax credit to be given to employers for each new employee hired.

If, in the early stages of a recession, every employer from General Motors to the corner filling station and local barber shop were given a tax credit of, for example, $200 a month for every new employee hired—adding to the work force in comparison to the preceeding year—a powerful incentive would be created for employers to add to their rolls rather than laying people off. Moreover, the government might well *save* money. The cost of every unemployed person, either in the form of unemployment insurance, Social Security, welfare, or food stamps is certainly in excess of $200, while at the same time the unemployed do not pay taxes. Thus, a tax subsidy to return these people to gainful employment would reduce their cost to the government by more than $200 and would also add their tax payments, both income and Social Security, to government revenues. With increased output, some of the corporate tax loss would also be recovered. Finally, by lowering labor costs, the employment tax credit would be antiinflationary.

To be sure, an employment tax credit would introduce distortions into the economy and would be hard on businesses that had no room for more labor. Imagine two barber shops, one with six chairs and six barbers, the other with six chairs but three barbers. The second would be able to hire three new barbers at a lower cost and could cut the price of a haircut. The first would have to scramble—perhaps by opening a massage parlor—to stay in business. For this reason, and because it is a countercyclical device, the proposed employment tax credit would have to be temporary, to be phased out gradually as full employment returned to the economy.[3]

A variant of this approach was proposed to the Joint Economic Committee of Congress by Professors Gary C. Fethke and Samuel H. Williamson of the University of Iowa. Called a "variable base employment credit," their scheme would permit a tax credit for workers hired in excess of a base level, but the base level would be adjusted to reflect changing business conditions. If a corporation normally employs one thousand people, then the tax credit would apply to any new workers hired above this "base" of one thousand. As the economy headed into a recession with rising unemployment, the base would gradually be lowered to, say, nine hundred. During boom times the base would be raised or the tax credit abolished.[4]

No matter what method is chosen, there will be distortions, extra paper work, cheating, and—as with every tax proposal—unfairness. When the employment tax credit was first discussed, the Secretary of the Treasury, W. Michael Blumenthal, complained that it would benefit expanding companies at the expense of companies that are not expanding. True enough, but it is the expanding companies that will pull the country out of a recession. Why not benefit them? (Blumenthal's argument could have been made—but was not—about the investment tax credit, introduced by the Kennedy Administration in the early 1960's.) Others, including the *Wall Street Journal* (editorial 12/22/75) and the *New York Times* (2/13/77) complained that it would take legions of bureaucrats to administer. Such need not be the case, so long as the tax credit is based upon payroll records, records which are at least as straightforward as the capital expenditure figures upon which the investment tax credit is calculated. Whatever the criticisms, the employment tax credit is a direct and inexpensive way to put people back to work. It will surely come up for reconsideration as unemployment once again becomes severe.

VOLUNTARY TEMPORARY UNEMPLOYMENT

The traditional policy solution for cyclical unemployment has been to increase unemployment benefits of one kind or another and/or to extend their duration. This, paradoxically, serves to increase the overall unemployment percentage, as people tend to take maximum advantage of their unemployment benefits before returning to work. A recent study by Professors Daniel Benjamin and Levis Kochin of the University of Washington analyzes the effect of unemployment benefits on unemployment in Great Britain between the years 1920 and 1938. Benjamin and Kochin conclude that over the entire period the unemployment insurance system, which was progressively liberalized, "raised the average unemployment by about five to eight percentage points."[5]

An interesting portion of this study reveals that during the years 1924–1935, when overall unemployment averaged 14.6%, the unemployment of juveniles aged 16 and 17 was only 5%. This unemployment rate jumped sharply at age 18 and again at 21. After carefully considering alternative explanations, the authors conclude that these increased unemployment rates *were caused by increased unemployment benefits at the higher age levels.*

This study by Benjamin and Kochin will probably become a classic, both because the statistical evidence is clear-cut and meticulously set forth and because it sheds an entirely different light on the conventional picture of a Britain between the wars stagnating in a sea of involuntary unemployment. The truth is that the growth in real income between the two wars equalled the most rapid growth ever achieved in a comparable period of time in British economic history.

But, one does not have to cross the Atlantic and go back 50 years to look at the effects of unemployment insurance on unemployment rates. Closer to home in time and place is a study of unemployment in Canada for the years 1953–1972 which concludes that "changes in the unemployment insurance scheme have substantially increased unemployment in recent years." The authors also found that increased unemployment insurance "creates incentives to join the labor force with the intention of working only temporarily."[6]

The unemployment begotten by unemployment insurance is largely temporary as well as voluntary, but it is, nonetheless, statistically counted as unemployment. If, for example, 20% of the labor force manages to stay unemployed three months out of the year, the statistical unemployment rate for the nation will be 5%.

Construction workers, substitute teachers, resort hotel employees, and many agricultural workers have part of their wages paid, in effect, by unemployment insurance. The employers in these and other seasonal industries are more willing to lay off workers when they are confident that these workers will return, while the workers don't mind being laid off because they know they will be recalled. Unemployment insurance during the layoff period reduces the cost to the employer and raises the benefits to the employee. It thus becomes an integral part of the wage calculation between the two—an untaxed wage supplement.

Professor Martin Feldstein of Harvard University concluded in 1978 that "the current average level of unemployment insurance benefits is responsible for approximately one-half of temporary layoff unemployment." The mutual benefit—to employer and employee—is borne out by Dr. Feldstein's finding that "temporary layoff unemployment is more than twice as frequent among union members as among others. . . ."[7] The high frequency of union members participating in this sort of arrangement hardly conveys a picture of government helping the weak and destitute.

So it is that unemployment insurance, begun as a policy response to the problem of cyclical unemployment, has embedded itself into the very pattern of American work habits. Its contribution to increasing the unemployment numbers resembles the contribution made by welfare. The difference is that unemployment insurance serves mainly to increase the frequency and duration of *temporary* unemployment, while welfare makes its mark by fostering *permanent* unemployment.

PERMANENT UNEMPLOYMENT

To the extent that temporary unemployment is the natural adaptation of consenting adults—employer and employee—to a government subsidy, it may be grounds for taxpayer indignation, but it is not a cause for humanitarian concern. However, permanent unemployment, even though it, too, is related to government subsidies, is a matter of deep concern. Whether voluntary or involuntary, it wreaks incalculable harm to those in its grip.

Government does its bit to raise permanent unemployment through welfare and the minimum wage. In 1977, when testifying in favor of an increase in the minimum wage, Labor Secretary Ray F. Marshall told Congress that *only* 90,000 people would be made jobless by that increase. This 90,000—the lowest "price tag" that the Administration dared put on its minimum wage increase legislation—looks like an innocent enough statis-

tic until one reflects that it represents the capacity of two Astrodomes. The Chamber of Commerce estimated the job loss at
840,000, or 18 Astrodomes-full. The truth may have lain
somewhere in between, say, ten Astrodomes, mostly full of
young people.

One of the arguments in favor of high minimum wages is
that these are needed to entice people away from the already
high levels of welfare.[8] This argument leads directly to the
intractible problem of the relationship between levels of welfare
payments and the unemployment that these payments themselves create. For, the fact is that a great many potential wage
earners will not find entry level jobs at wages sufficiently high
to forgo the leisure (or the "off-the-books," "subterranean,"
"barter," or "for cash only" activities) that welfare affords.

Dr. Martin Anderson of the Hoover Institution, Stanford
University, describes this as a "poverty wall," forcing welfare
recipients to pay "marginal tax rates" of 80% or more in order
to become employed.[9] A marginal tax rate is the amount of
pennies per dollar that the government gets (or in this case
takes back) from each *additional* dollar of earnings. We usually
think of high marginal tax rates in terms of high income brackets. Currently, someone making $50,000 or more pays 50%
Federal income tax on each additional dollar that he or she
earns. But, as Anderson points out, an unemployed man in
New Jersey with a wife and two children on welfare would add
only $110 to his net monthly income if he took a full-time job
paying $500 a month. Furthermore, he would lose his eligibility
for medicaid! This means that for every dollar he earned ("additional" to not working at all) the government would get 78
cents. Is such a meagre prospect of personal gain worth giving
up fishing, or working on a neighbor's house in return for
unspecified services, or selling heroin on the streets, or writing
a book, or planning bank robberies? It is probably a mistake to
think of those on welfare as indolent, but it is certainly not a
mistake to believe that they are just as capable of calculating
their own self-interest as is anybody else.

In effect the United States income tax structure (the marginal tax rate on each additional dollar of income—or day
worked) places the heaviest burden on the *lowest* end of the
earning spectrum. If the 50% tax rates on upper bracket in-

come already tend to encourage resort to barter, tax cheating, and other "off the books" activities, imagine the encouragements given by the 80% tax rates at the bottom!

This can scarcely have been the intent of those who designed (if the word can be used) our welfare programs. Is there any reform that would solve the problem and be politically acceptable? The answer seems to be no. Experts in the field, in and out of government, have been working without success for well over a decade to reconcile three mutually incompatible goals: adequate levels of welfare, reasonable budget cost, and strong incentives to work. Any two of the goals are attainable at any time, but all three cannot be reached simultaneously. If you combine adequate welfare benefits with adequate incentives to work, then you must continue to pay welfare to families whose members start working, and, in fairness, these benefits must be extended to all the working poor. This would send the cost of welfare out of sight. If you try to keep the budget cost of welfare within limits, yet maintain an incentive to work, then welfare benefits must be slashed to levels that are morally unacceptable.

It might be added that if you try to solve the incentive problem by raising the minimum wage, then you cause a huge increase in unemployment, and you send all wage levels skyward. There are simply no easy answers. What answers there are boil down to more effective policing of welfare programs: setting work requirements, eliminating fraud, etc. Even these measures will tend to raise costs. Anderson's best suggestion is to turn the administration of welfare programs over to the states, cities, and towns which are closer to the people receiving their benefits (and, one might add, to the people paying for them), more knowledgeable about the local situation and, one hopes, more hard-headed about abuses.

YOUTH UNEMPLOYMENT

The area of unemployment that is most destructive to society is youth unemployment. In the United States the unemployment rate among youths runs between 15% and 20%, and youth unemployment accounts for more than 40% of total unemployment. The youth unemployment problem has also struck

Europe, with unemployment rates for the same age group
ranging from 5.5% in Germany to 9.2% in France, not yet as
high as the United States but far higher than it used to be and
far higher than the concurrent overall unemployment rates in
these countries.[10]

Youth unemployment is in part the result of a host of cul-
tural factors beyond the purview of this book, such as the
emergence of television as a competitor to formal education,
the failure of the schools themselves to supply useful training,
and the decay of the family as an institution. For the rest, the
chief culprit is the minimum wage law, which raises the cost of
youth training programs and obliges employers either to look
for mature experienced workers, who will be worth the cost of
the minimum wage, or simply to do without the additional
labor.

One of the most tragic impacts of the minimum wage has
been on the unemployment rate of young blacks in this country. Today, black youth unemployment is 40% versus 16% for
white youths, *and* participation in the labor force by these blacks
is only half that of whites (the rest having given up trying).
However, in 1948, black youth unemployment was 9.4%—*lower*
than the 10.4% rate for young whites, while black youth participation in the labor force was 8% higher! Has this dramatic
change in the relative positions of black and white youths been
due to an *increase* in racial discrimination over the past 30 years?
Has it been due to a *decrease* in the skills that black youths have
to offer? Both answers seem unlikely, and Professor Walter E.
Williams of Temple University argues that job opportunites for
black youths as compared with white have shrunk because of
legislated increases in the minimum wage and extensions of its
coverage.[11]

Any exemption for youth from the minimum wage has been
forcefully opposed by organized labor. Here one can only wonder at the dearth of creative thinking among labor leaders.
Aside from the responsibility which they share with the rest of
society for the training of new generations, there is the opportunity, thus far missed, to coopt these generations into the labor
movement. Cleverly designed apprenticeship programs under
union guidance—with a carefully controlled waiver of the
minimum wage—would guarantee a source of well-

indocrinated new membership, and perhaps even serve as an entering wedge to organize nonunion industries and areas.

Until the Labor Gerontocracy sees the light of its own self-interest, let alone its social responsibility, there is little likelihood of an exemption from the minimum wage in favor of the young. Therefore, other solutions must be found, inevitably involving some government subsidy, either in the form of federally financed job programs or incentives to private industry to employ more youth.

The first of these alternatives is by far the most costly. One authoritative estimate made three years ago calculated the cost of a federal jobs program at $18,000 per person employed, including start-up costs and the bureaucracy necessary to do the administration.[12] Today that cost would be well over $25,000, and one doubts that tax-paying 30-year-old college graduates or even Ph.D.s earning less than $25,000 would relish seeing their tax dollars spent this way. The cost in human terms would be far higher. In the name of social justice, Congress would inevitably decree that any federal jobs program pay at least the minimum wage and probably the "prevailing" wage rate in the area. This would ensure that there was no incentive to leave the federal program, whose participants would thus be surrounded by the gilded walls of a government ghetto, coddled within them, but deprived of any incentive to join the mainstream of society. Such a program amounts to a prison without bars. Sweeping the underprivileged under the rug, it assuages our social guilt, while condemning the "beneficiaries" to permanent isolation.

The second alternative is a subsidy to make private industry create jobs for youth. This can take two forms. One is a direct cash subsidy to private industry. A bill providing for such subsidies was introduced in the Senate in 1979 by Senators Bentson, Chafee, Danforth, Kennedy, and McGovern. It contains elaborate provisions regarding the eligibility of youths for which the government will pay: family income, length of prior unemployment, etc., and even more elaborate performance requirements on the part of the employer in order to qualify for the subsidy. This well-intentioned effort conjures up visions of a new nursing home scandal: ingenious "businessmen" will set up programs to collect the latest federal cornucopia; a bribeable bureaucracy will administer the largesse, and the victims will be the nation's youth and the nation's taxpayers.

The other form of subsidy for private employment of younger workers is a tax credit, similar to the employment tax credit advocated earlier in this chapter. Contrary to a direct subsidy, a tax credit benefits firms that are already making money. This has the effect of steering youths into areas which offer the most opportunity.

Furthermore, the tax credit should be administered purely on the basis of the numbers employed, not on the basis of their race, family income, previous unemployment, education, physical disabilities, sex, or other arbitrary criteria. This approach will inevitably attract criticism that it fails to help the *most* disadvantaged and that employers might get a tax credit for employing persons they would have employed anyway, but on the other hand it spares us the creation of a brand new bureaucracy to administer the rules of eligibility. It may be likened to the action of a pump reducing the whole pool of unemployed rather than a ladle dipping in to fish out specific beneficiaries. In the long run, a pump is much more effective than a ladle.

Compassion and common sense require that we make every possible effort to reduce unemployment to a minimum. Unemployment costs money and wrecks lives. However, the traditional solutions to this problem have not worked in recent years. Fiscal and monetary stimulation have produced inflation without cutting significantly into unemployment.

Instead, carefully designed tax policies deserve a try: for cyclical unemployment, a temporary tax credit, to be phased out as boom times return; for youth unemployment, a permanent tax credit program.

11

THE PURSUIT OF THE PLUPERFECT

Definition of a Consumer: Someone who is qualified to elect a President but not competent to purchase a bicycle without the aid of a Federal Agency.

HERBERT STEIN, *former Chairman, President's Council of Economic Advisors*

The Constitution opens with a solecism that expresses a deep trait in the American character: "In order to form a more perfect union. . . ." Perfection, itself never to be achieved on earth, is insufficient for Americans. No matter how good things are, they can be made more perfect, if only we try hard enough. Like any commendable ambition the pursuit of more perfection can be carried to extremes, as has been done by enthusiastic Congresses over the past fifteen years. Here is a partial list of the "more perfections" decreed by legislation since 1965:

A more perfect environment
More perfect product safety
More perfect health
More perfect worker safety
More perfect employment and promotion opportunity
  by race
  by sex
  by age
  by language
  by handicap
  by veteran status

More perfect pension fund protection

More perfect financial disclosure

More perfect product labeling and advertising

More perfect description of the terms on which loans are made

More perfect competition

And last, but not least, more perfect human moral conduct.

No right-minded person will dispute the proposition that it would be nice to reach and even surpass perfection in each one of these goals. At the same time, sensible readers will wonder whether achievement of all of these greater perfections is possible without setting priorities. More than that, are these goals compatible with another goal that cannot be legislated: the survival of our free society? To restate the old saw about ends and means, the survival of a democracy is imperiled when its people become so seduced by the chimerae of absolute goals, that they no longer take note of the means being used to achieve them.

The means to achieve more perfection are as varied as the government agents—over 80,000—who have been given the power to regulate. Here are just a few examples.

One company's plant was visited by a team of inspectors from the Occupational Safety and Health Administration (OSHA), which ordered that the washroom facilities for female employees include a lounge where the women could sit and wait, if necessary. Compliance with this order provoked a directive from the Equal Employment Opportunity Commission (EEOC) insisting that the women's lounge constitutes discrimination against male employees and must be dismantled unless comparable facilities are built for the men.[1]

To protect workers from noise pollution OSHA demanded that the steel industry introduce engineering that would involve a capital cost of $1.2 million for each worker affected, rather than do a better job with ear protectors at the cost of $42 per employee.[2]

When the Environmental Protection Agency (EPA) ruled in 1975 that operators of grain elevators could not allow grain dust to escape into the atmosphere, the incidence of major grain elevator explosions rose to thirteen per year from an average of eight in prior years. If grain dust is not vented, it becomes explosive.²

Two years after enactment by Congress of the Employee Retirement Income Security Act of 1974, 7,300 pension plans were *terminated*. The paper work necessary to comply with ERISA regulations was just too much for smaller companies. As for the managers of the pension funds that remained in existence, the new Federal standards forced substitution of bureaucratic caution for honest investment judgment, to the ultimate detriment of the pension fund beneficiaries. Professor Murray Weidenbaum of George Washington University, St. Louis, the source of most of these anecdotes, notes that the Social Security program would not come close to meeting actuarial and other requirements imposed by Congress on private pension funds.²

In January, 1977, the Dow Chemical Company cancelled plans for building a $300 million petrochemical complex in California to meet West Coast demand. Comments Dow's President, "After more than two years and costs exceeding $4 million for an environmentally sound project, we hadn't even reached first base in the regulatory red tape maze." The story of Dow's investment cancellation can be retold hundreds of times by executives in almost every area.²

Research has also suffered. According to the head of General Motors' Research Laboratory, "We've diverted a large share of our resources—something up to half—into meeting government regulations instead of developing better materials, better manufacturing techniques, and better products. . . . It's a terrible way to waste your research dollars."²

The sad story of the Chrysler Corporation is an example of how the simultaneous pursuit of two or more perfections can lead to disaster. In the decade from 1965 to 1975 the automobile industry was saddled with three successive sets of regulation: first was the issue of safety, under the prodding of Ralph Nader. Next, pollution came to the fore, and, finally, after the 1974 oil price increase, fuel consumption standards were set. Meeting these three regulatory barrages required from each automobile manufacturer a heavy lump-sum investment in research and development. Any sane government would have allowed, indeed encouraged, the companies to pool their research, but this was ruled out, presumably on the grounds that it would be counter to the goal of more perfect competition. So, each company was obliged to go its own way, developing its own response to the requirements of safety, clean air, and miles-per-gallon regulation. Obviously, the fewer cars produced, the greater the regulatory research and development per car. Chrysler, as the smallest of the Big Three, bears the brunt. The company's estimated cost of meeting regulations over an eight-year span from 1978 through 1985 comes to $800 million per year, less in total amount than the $2 billion a year estimated by General Motors, but nonetheless $550 per car produced versus $345 per GM car. This is how companies go bankrupt in the name of more perfect safety, more perfect air to breathe, more perfect conservation of energy, and, of course, more perfect competition.[3]

The estimated total cost of Federal regulation of the nation's business is about $100 billion a year, of which $5 billion is direct government cost in administering the regulations and $95 billion the cost to industry of complying with them.* This regulatory burden has the same effect as a direct profits tax on corporations, except that there is no revenue generated. As was pointed out in earlier chapters, taxes paid by corporations must ultimately be paid by individuals, be they consumers, employees, or shareholders. In short, the corporate tax is a concealed method of taxing individuals—mainly consumers—without telling them. By the same token, government regulation is a way of making consumers pay for social goals, some of them important, some of them fanciful, without being aware that it is they who are paying. By now the estimated cost of government regulation is $20 billion more per year than the total tax paid by corporations and double the taxes paid by manufacturing corporations. If every consumer were obliged to pay separately for the regulatory cost of every product that he or she buys, government regulation would be streamlined fast.

---

*This $100 billion estimate was made by Professor Weidenbaum and Robert De Fina of the Center for Study of American Business at George Washington University, St. Louis. It has been hotly attacked by Mark Green, a Nader associate (see *New York Times*, October 28, 1979, p. 18f), who does not offer an alternate estimate. The Office of Management and Budget (OMB) estimated total costs of regulation in 1975 at between $113.3 and 135.4 billion. The General Accounting Office (GAO) concluded that OMB's estimate was significantly overstated, but came up with no alternate.

In addition to this direct regulatory burden of \$100 billion—\$25 billion of it for paperwork alone—there is the burden of litigation that arises out of the laws and rules governing business operations. No estimate has been made of these costs to the public.

Finally, there is a cost that cannot be quantified—the cost to our freedom. When this cost causes extreme personal inconvenience to large numbers of people, including Congressmen themselves, as in the case of the automobile interlock device, then there is enough protest to force revision of the regulations. When only a few are hurt, as in the case of drugs that the FDA will not clear, then there might be some temporary publicity, but nothing is done. More often Americans will simply not know about drugs, readily available in other countries, that might save their lives or make those lives more endurable.

So much for the consumer impact of unfettered regulation. What happens to the freedoms of the inventor, the entrepreneur, and the producer? The tiny tip of this iceberg can be described in the few indiscrete remarks that have been made in public by government regulators over the decade:

> "If a company violates our statute, we will not concern ourselves with its middle level executives; we will put the chief executive in jail. Once we put a top executive behind bars, I am sure we will get a much higher degree of compliance from other companies." Richard O. Simpson, Chairman, CPSC, 1972.[1]

> "We do not pay any attention to the economic consequences of our decisions." J. Richard Crout, Director FDA Bureau of Drugs, 1975.[2]

> "It is very difficult for a company that did not start hiring yesterday—literally yesterday—not to be in violation." Eleanor Holmes Norton, head of EEOC, 1978.[2]

> "This will give a lot of business to a lot of lawyers." A member of the Federal Trade Commission, 1978.[2]

> "People often eat for the wrong reasons." An FTC official, 1978.[2]

One can only imagine what is said in private. If any such remarks were made publicly by an official of the FBI commenting on antinuclear demonstrators, the media uproar would be instantaneous. These remarks have lain buried in business publications or regional newspapers, awaiting disinternment by Dr. Weidenbaum.[2]

Our legislators' zeal for the pluperfect may have reached its apogee in the enactment of the nobly named "Foreign Corrupt Practices Act of 1977," which, for the first time in the history of American criminal law, makes an act conceived and executed in a foreign country a criminal offense over here. To do in Rome as the Romans do means criminal prosecution in Washington. As three academic experts point out, proper enforcement of this particular law will require electronic and physical surveillance of scores of United States civilians in nations throughout the world.[4] Ironically, a Congress that was appalled at the idea of surveillance of any United States citizen who might be working for Soviet Intelligence, seems to have been charmed by the thought of monitoring the activities of American corporate executives who might attempt to beat out Japanese (or French or German) competitors by paying customary bribes in third countries. The cost of this legislation to United States exports was conservatively estimated by the Carter Administration (which supported it but may now be having second thoughts) at one billion dollars a year. In the words of Congressman Bob Eckhardt of Texas, "Maybe it's worth that to keep America honest."[5] Cynics may ask what it is worth to keep Congress honest.

Bribery is normally considered to be wrong, though it has existed in every civilization the world has ever known. Indeed, many observers have pointed out that the more socialist an economy is, the more bribery (including "pull" and black markets) becomes necessary to make it function.[6,7] The foreign Corrupt Practices Act will not stamp out bribery worldwide. What it will do is establish the basis for worldwide harassment of American citizens by their government.

Development of the freedoms that we enjoy today has roughly paralleled development of the industrial economies of the Western World. Most of the philosophical thought that guided the evolution of these freedoms, including that of John Stuart Mill, John Locke, David Hume, and the framers of our Constitution, has revolved around the freedom of ideas and their expression. Even the relationship of economics, e.g., capitalism, to freedom has been discussed only in general terms, under the proposition that the free market is essential to all other freedoms. Not until recently has freedom for the creator of *products* rather than *ideas* become a specific issue. The freedom to invent a new product and to produce and market it with some reasonable chance of success is just as important to inventors and producers as the freedom to express ideas is to writers. It goes without saying that the freedom of invention and production is of vital importance to society.

To this writer, one of the extremes of unjustified harassment is the mandate granted by Congress to the FDA to oblige pharmaceutical companies to prove, at great cost, that each new drug is not only harmless but *positively beneficial*. Is it really the function of a bureaucrat to dispute the psychological benefit of snake oil?

None of this is a plea for the abolition of all government regulation. Regulation is necessary to protect third parties and society as a whole in cases where there is obviously no mechanism within the free market itself that provides such protection. In the case of snake oil by any other name, consumers will sooner or later decide that it is not worth their shrinking dollars and will stop buying it. Herbert Stein's witticism, quoted at the beginning of this chapter, expresses a common but gallingly patronizing attitude on the part of many "intellectuals" and politicians: that the very people upon whose votes the fate of our democracy rests must be protected from their own stupidity when they turn around and buy a bicycle.

The dumping of toxic wastes is a different matter. The free market has no mechanism for protecting the environment in which we live. Specifically, if Company A is freely dumping its refuse into the water or into the air, then Company B, its competitor, cannot simply decide to be a good citizen and still survive. The extra costs for properly processing and disposing of the same wastes would soon bankrupt it. Government regulation preserves the competitive balance between both and enables each, together with the rest of us, to survive. Regulation is a subject which needs to be approached with common sense rather than with fanaticism, pro or anti.

Unfortunately, zealots tend to gravitate towards the regulatory agencies and especially towards the self-appointed citizens

groups that prod these agencies. A Consumers' Committee for Common Sense would, alas, never enlist the energies of a Ralph Nader or a Jane Fonda. Such people need both an absolute cause to love and an impersonal institution to hate. The safest and most satisfying cause to love is "mankind" or "consumers"; the pet hate institution used to be called "big business," but in these more sophisticated days the "multinational corporation" somehow sounds better. So long as the Naders and Fondas and the people who follow them fail to remember that "mankind" and "multinational corporations" are both made up of human beings, with human virtues and faults, then neither compromise nor common sense will be easy to find.

Yet, it is towards compromise and common sense that we must grope. Regulation deserves neither a pedestal nor a meat axe. While there is no snap solution to the problem, it is to be hoped that once people realize just who is paying for all the regulations designed to protect us, moderation will out. For, whether we are called "mankind" or "consumers" or just plain voters, it is we and not some big bad corporation who must foot the bill in the end.

REGULATING WAGES AND PRICES

A more fanciful, but happily more intermittent, instance of governmental intervention into our lives is the imposition of wage and price controls. At various times since World War II nearly every Western free market society, including ours, has attempted to slap on such controls. They have never worked, but the dream lives on. Almost any public opinion poll taken during a period of inflation will show support for wage and price controls as a seemingly simple remedy for the pocketbook pain of inflation. If only because of this perennial appeal to those with short memories, the workings of such direct controls deserve analysis.

The purpose of price controls, obviously, is to force producers to sell their goods at a lower price than they could otherwise get in a free market. In most cases this can be done—for a while. If, however, the same goods can be sold in another country for a price higher than the controlled price, they will be, and immediate shortages will develop at home. The longer-run effect of price controls is that production of each controlled item will drop to a lower level than that which could have been produced at uncontrolled prices. Again, shortages will develop. The shortages will require, first, allocation (a polite term for rationing) then rationing (a less polite term for allocation).

Wage controls are, for the United States and Japan, easier to administer than price controls, because workers cannot readily move abroad in search of higher, uncontrolled wages. However, in Europe even wage controls can present a problem, unless a nation, like East Germany, is willing to use guns, fences, and dogs to keep its work force in place. The Dutch wage control system was lauded by bankers in Amsterdam in the early 1960's as a model of economic cleverness. Employers were not allowed to increase wages unless they could prove that there had been an increase in productivity. This suited the Dutch banks fine, because they could not possibly prove that they were increasing productivity, and, therefore, they didn't have to pass out pay raises. One of the reasons why the Dutch wage controls collapsed, however, was that too many workers could bicycle or take the bus across the border to Germany and receive the free market rate for their labor.

This brief description of how wage and price controls do and do not work is intended to emphasize that the difficulty is not deciding to impose them, but rather deciding when, how, and whether to take them off again. Left on, they require an ever broader system of rationing, and may even culminate in government restraint on personal movement so as to keep workers employed in "essential," i.e., the most controlled, industries. Of all non-Marxian economists, only Professor John Kenneth Galbraith seems to advocate a permanent system of wage and price controls.

Professor Galbraith loves to point out that during World War II wage and price controls were remarkably successful. Their success was due to two reasons: they were a necessary part of the "war effort" and they were temporary. In those days, evaders were known as "black marketeers," and were shunned socially. In 1980, however, who is prepared to predict the public reaction to the plight of a seven-foot basketball player who cannot negotiate himself an extra quarter of a million dollars for a year's toil?

Above all, the fact that controls and rationing were a part of the war effort implied a termination date—the end of the war—so that people could cooperate, knowing that they would not be saddled with them forever.

It is a safe bet that when people who are polled respond enthusiastically in favor of wage and price controls, they have in mind some sort of quick fix whereby controls would miraculously end inflation, after which they could be removed. The question "Are you in favor of wage and price controls and rationing for the rest of your lives?" might get quite a different answer.

What about a quick fix? Controls have never worked in the post-War period, but there is a reason for that. Wage and price controls are like a corset on a lady. A corset is cosmetic. It is painful, yet it boosts morale. If the lady dons the corset and simultaneously follows a strict low-calorie regimen—slimming beneath the stays—she can eventually consign the uncomfortable garment to the closet as a useful reminder of the perils of dietary excess. However, if she continues to eat chocolates, she will begin to bulge around the edges, and finally the corset will burst. It will be discredited.

Such has invariably been the case with wage and price controls. Politicians held the belief that once these controls were firmly in place it would be quite safe to inflate the economy, mainly by printing and distributing money. However, bulges, which economists call "dislocations," inevitably appeared, and at length the controls failed or had to be abandoned. The Nixon controls are a case in point. If they had not been removed, they would assuredly have burst in the face of soaring food prices, soaring oil prices, and soaring prices for nearly everything else, due to the printing of chocolate money by the Federal Reserve System.

This experience suggests that if controls were to be imposed in the form of an across-the-board freeze of limited duration, then they could serve as useful shock therapy, giving more fundamental antiinflation measures time to take effect. Much of this book has been given over to the psychological problem of money terror—the universal anticipation of inflation against

Wage and price controls . . .

which no one can protect him- or herself. When these fears become deep-rooted, as by now they are, then strictly "economic" measures, including money and credit restraint and a change in tax policy to encourage investment rather than consumption, may be swept away by a wave of popular panic before they have a chance to succeed. A cooling period in a deep freeze of wages and prices, for anywhere from 6 to 18 months, would give everyone a chance to assess the inflation problem and moderate their demands. With a policy package that included both the corset *and* the diet, the pressure on prices would be minimal, because the dollar would rise in the foreign exchange markets, making most internationally traded commodities cheaper rather than more expensive in dollar terms.

A quick freeze on wages and prices stands a good chance of success because it combines shock, drama, and brevity. Introduced by a strong administration, it would undoubtedly be politically popular.

This is not the case with wage-price guidelines, which have justly earned labor mistrust and voter derision. Guidelines inevitably become minimums, not maximums, floors rather than ceilings. What labor leader would dare come away from the bargaining table with *less* than the government-guidelined increase? As for producers, even if the market is momentarily weak, it makes little sense to raise prices less than the guidelines allow, for when and if demand picks up again, the lower price may well be the base for the next increase. The psychology of guidelines is very much like that of departmental budget allocations within government. Department chiefs hasten to spend their full budget by the end of the fiscal year to avoid a cutback in appropriations for the next year.

Every guideline that offers "breathing room" for annual increases in wages and prices is an artificial respirator, pumping continued inflation into the economy.

12

A SURVIVAL KIT
FOR CAPITALISM

Lenin was certainly right. There is no subtler, no surer means of
overturning the existing basis of Society than to debauch the
currency. The process engages all the hidden forces of economic
law on the side of destruction and does it in a manner which not
one man in a million is able to diagnose.

JOHN MAYNARD KEYNES

CURRENCY CONFIDENCE

In the months before August 15, 1971, when the United States
led the world off the gold exchange standard, officials at the
Treasury Department periodically attended day-long seminars,
wherein 15 to 20 of the nation's top economists offered their
considered opinions on the proper course to be taken to defend
the dollar in a hostile world. These sessions were interrupted
for a frugal sandwich lunch, but their content was a far-from-
frugal diet for the mind.

It was at one of these that the phrase "benign neglect of the
dollar" surfaced in official circles. This catchy phrase summarized a complicated idea: if other countries, such as Germany and Japan, continued to sell more goods to the United
States than they bought from it, they would be obliged either to
absorb the dollars that they earned from these surpluses or to
revalue their own currencies. If they absorbed the dollars, their
bank reserves would expand subjecting them to a domestic inflation that would price their exports out of the market. If, on
the other hand, they elected to revalue their currencies, their
exports would again rise in price, with the same result. Here
was a neat, automatic formula. We go our way and other countries must adjust, either by inflating or revaluing. As it turned

out, neither revaluation (by Germany) nor inflation (in Japan) caused these countries to lose their trade advantage, which shows that even the best of theories can be confounded by events.

Nevertheless, benign neglect of the dollar was a popular idea among a broad spectrum of economists—from Keynesian to Monetarist—and its logical conclusion, a floating rate international monetary system, remains equally popular today in most academic circles. Floating exchange rates allow countries to neglect the value of their currencies in either direction: those who want less inflation can print less money and let their currencies float upwards; those who want more can flood themselves and the world with their currencies and float downwards. Floating rates, it is argued, provide wide latitude for domestic monetary policy by removing the need for concern over the balance of payments.

In actuality, floating rates completely eliminated monetary stimulation as a policy tool. As pointed out in Chapter 4, if the President decreed that anyone with one dollar in his pocket, or his bank, could receive another dollar from the government for free, there would be no stimulation of the economy. The only net effect would be a doubling of all prices and a halving of the currency's value abroad. This is an extreme example of our nation's experience during the 1970's. When the Federal Reserve increased the money supply in large doses, foreign exchange dealers marked the dollar down; producers marked their prices up; workers demanded cost-of-living pay increases. Only *savers* were left holding the bag, for the Fed did not give *them* a "free dollar" for every dollar they had saved. The only way they could protect themselves was to demand higher interest rates for the money they lent out. Thus, interest rates inevitably rose.

Did all this money printing stimulate the economy? The answer is probably yes, but in a very unhealthy fashion. Money terror caused a flight from the dollar not only into gold, commodities, and foreign currencies but also into houses, cars, and any other goods consumers could lay their hands on. This consumer terror over inflation buoyed up the economy more than any government budgetary policy. Government deficits, lumping the federal deficit together with the surpluses of states and municipalities, have been negligible compared to consumer borrowing which increased at a rate approaching $150 billion dollars a year. The result might be called a successful Keynesian depression, with savings and investment falling to abysmally low levels, while the economy enjoyed the false prosperity of consuming its own tissue.

As this book goes to press a determined Federal Reserve Board of Governors under new leadership has taken strong steps to restore public confidence, here and abroad, in the currency. Specifically, it has pledged that regardless of the effect on interest rates, the money supply will be restrained. The pain that the Fed's actions may cause will be directly inverse to the speed and degree that the Fed is believed. If people believe that, after a decade of vacillation and in an election year, the Fed will stick to its guns, then interest rates will decline.

Should, on the other hand, people continue to doubt that the Fed will—*or can*—control the amount of dollars created by the banking system, then interest rates will continue to rise, and the economy will be in serious trouble. *Restoration of confidence in the currency is the essential precondition for full employment and economic growth.*

THE COMING INVESTMENT BOOM

But there is more ot it than that. Restoration of confidence in the dollar would lay the groundwork for one of the greatest investment booms in our nation's history. Once people are assured that the United States Government is determined to avoid any increase in the quantity of dollars floating around this country and the rest of the world, the dollar will rise in the exchange markets and the inflation premium, which has largely caused today's high level of interest rates, will disappear. Falling interest rates will give the financial markets an enormous shot in the arm. The market value of long-term debt in the hands of the public—pension funds, insurance companies, mutual funds, banks, and individual savers—amounts to some $800 billion. The average interest rate on this debt is close to 11%. During noninflationary periods of moderate growth that this country has seen in the past, the long-term interest rate has averaged less than 5%, which suggests that more than half of the current interest rate represents an inflation premium. If this is squeezed out—through a credible commitment to stop printing money—the market value of these savings will increase in a rough order of magnitude from $800 billion to $1.1 trillion. Such a rise in the bond market will—other things being equal—spill over into the stock market, creating both the means and the desire for business expansion.

Thus, there is reasonable ground to believe that curtailing the growth of the money supply will ultimately result in expansion rather than recession. There is another reason for this optimistic view. A return of confidence in the dollar, coupled with rising financial markets in this country, will attract massive flows of foreign money for investment in American stocks and bonds. Badly as our economy has been managed, it is still the largest and politically most attractive investment opportunity in the world. Savings rates have been extremely high abroad, both in Europe and particularly in some of the oil producing nations. This money is poised to rush over here as soon as confidence in the dollar and the United States economy can be justified.

To be sure, one could take an apocalyptic view. There are as many things wrong with our society as there are writers to point them out. We consume too much and save too little. Our investment rate is far too low. There is probably too much consumer debt and too much government debt outstanding. There may be, as President Carter maintains, the beginnings of a sense of hopelessness—"*malaise*"—in the land. All of these ills are intimately linked with inflationary psychology. When people know that the value of their money is rapidly declining, then saving makes no sense, and consumption becomes an act of desperation. The Last Meal is eaten with grim gusto and without hope for the morrow.

A WAGE-PRICE FREEZE

The Federal Reserve System under Paul Volcker has set about to remedy this. If its efforts are of themselves insufficient to dispel money terror, then the shock therapy of a temporary wage-price freeze deserves a try. At this point it is very likely that a wage-price freeze would be politically popular for a short while. Polls have indicated a public yen for wage and price controls as a seemingly painless way to get rid of inflation. A dramatic freeze would stir the public imagination and at the same time provide a cooling-off period for ongoing wage negotiations. As has been pointed out, a wage-price freeze could only be effective if stringent monetary policies to control inflation were pursued at the same time. This would be in sharp contrast to every other instance of peacetime wage and price controls. Every nation that tried them abused them by pumping up purchasing power to the point where the controls burst.

TAXES AND GROWTH

While steps are taken to eliminate inflation, growth and employment can be restored as well. Today, even members of Congress have discovered that investment is necessary for growth, productivity, and employment. Investment can be made possible only through changes in the lax laws that currently siphon off investment money. Today some major American corporations are taxed at levels that exceed 100% of their true profits. They are consuming their assets in order to survive. The overall tax rate on nonfinancial corporations, if one allows for the eventual replacement of their assets at inflated prices, is well in excess of 50%.

In Chapter 8 it was demonstrated in detail that the corporate profits tax is mainly paid by consumers, and that a sales tax would be more honest. A sales tax would also be more efficient. Debate has just begun in this country on the advisability of importing a European tax device called the Value Added Tax, or VAT. The VAT is a glorified sales tax.* As proposed by Mr. Al Ullman, Chairman of the House Ways and Means Committee, it would bring in $130 billion a year, and politicians are already looking for ways to put this money into the hands of

---

*The Value Added Tax (VAT) is an uniquely European institution. According to Professor Melvin Krauss of New York University, it was first introduced in France, because retailers there couldn't be relied upon to collect a sales tax. The VAT is a tax levied on each stage of the production process: logs to pulp mill, pulp to paper, paper to author, author to book, book to reader. Each processor adds his "value," but each has been obliged to pay the fellow before him, and therefore makes sure that he is in turn paid by the one after. It is a marvellous way of making sure that the French pay their taxes, and, who knows? might well be useful over here.

consumers by cutting individual income and social security taxes. Thus, under the Ullman formula there would be a $130 billion increase in consumer prices and a $130 billion increase in consumer after-tax incomes in order to pay the higher prices. This is hardly the way to fight inflation.

However, if a VAT of only $70 billion were levied and used to replace all corporate profits taxes (which amount to roughly $70 billion), the effect on prices would be minimal in the short run and highly beneficial over the long term. This book has laid repeated stress not only on the need for greater investment but also on the need for more efficient allocation of that investment. The central problem of economic management is to allocate resources smoothly and efficiently. In the Soviet Union this is done by a central planning board. In the United States it is done by the free market and in particular by the financial markets. Substitution of a VAT for the corporate profits tax would make this process vastly speedier and more efficient.

Taking two hypothetical companies, this is how it would work. Consolidated Conduit, Inc. is making lead pipe in a plant that is 50 years old; it earns $10 million on $100 million in sales and pays taxes of $5 million. Digestotronics, Inc. is marketing a product that will prepare home-cooked take-out meals using solar energy and requiring no human effort in the cooking or clean-up; it earns $20 million on sales of $100 million and pays $10 million in taxes. If the 50% profits tax is replaced by a flat 7½% VAT, the Government will get the same $15 million from the two companies, but Digestotronics will have $12.5 million instead of $10 million with which to expand, while Consolidated will have only $2.5 million. Investment money will be attracted towards Digestotronics to the ultimate benefit of the working homemaker, though perhaps not of the family palate. Consolidated Conduit will fade away.

Substitution of a VAT for the corporate income tax would tend to speed the flow of the nation's resources into areas of high technology and high productivity, a development that is essential if the United States is to maintain, let alone increase, living standards and international competitiveness. This substitution would—until other countries caught on and follows suit—make the United States the most attractive country for high-technology investment, with a corresponding impact on employment and productivity.

PERSONAL INCOME TAXES

The corporate income tax is not the only area where enormous progress could be made if only stale ideologies and prejudices were overcome. The *personal* income tax rises to 50% on earned income, but to 70% if investment income—that is, the income earned from savings—is added. There is general agreement that individual savings and investment should, somehow, be stimulated, but the present tax laws penalize savings, and work to channel investment into relatively useless tax shelters.

A recent study made by W.R. Grace and Company[1] estimates that a reduction in personal income tax rates from a maximum of 70% to a maximum of 36% would cost the Treasury only $7.5 billion. This estimate strongly suggests that personal income tax rates in the United States are well above the URP point on the Laffer Curve. Reducing these rates would result in more work and more efficient investment, which would soon recoup the initial loss to the Treasury.

However, it is very difficult, politically and morally, to reduce tax rates on the "rich," even if reducing the *rates* would increase the actual *revenues*.

It is for this reason that I recommend imposition of a wealth tax of 1% per annum on net financial and real estate assets. Such a tax would bring in an estimated $15 billion (all of these estimates should be taken with a large grain of salt; they are very rough orders of magnitude). That would be more than enough to offset the immediate loss in revenue from lowered rates of personal income tax in the higher brackets on those who must earn their money. Most important, a wealth tax would ensure that the established rich made an appropriate contribution, while not destroying the incentives and opportunities for those who are still trying to become rich.

THE CAPITAL GAINS TAX

A further way to increase tax revenues and increase the efficiency of investment allocation would be to reduce the capital gains tax. This tax is levied on transactions—sales of assets—that are usually optional. Studies (already cited) indicate that if this tax rate were reduced, the number of taxable transactions would increase and actual tax collections would rise. At the same time, a lower capital gains tax rate—for example, a maximum of 10%—would enable individuals to move their savings more rapidly from less productive investments to more productive ones. This would help greatly to free the flow of capital, especially into the new enterprises upon which the nation's future must depend.

Looking optimistically into the picture, if an investment boom does indeed take place in the United States, there will come a time when that boom, like all booms, is carried to excess. At such a time, an increase in the capital gains tax would gently quiet investor enthusiasm without precipitating a sudden crash. The policy uses of taxation are infinite.

The sum of these suggested tax changes—a 1% wealth tax, a 36% maximum personal income tax, and a 10% maximum capital gains tax—would, with virtual certainty, produce more tax revenue than the present structure. In other words, it would soak the rich more effectively than we do today. At the same time, it would do much less damage to the economy: there would be far less diversion of money into tax shelters; the incentive for actual tax avoidance would be reduced, as would the incentive for barter and other "off the books" activity. The free flow of investment into areas where it is needed would be greatly facilitated. Finally, the voters could be assured, for the first time, that no rich man (or woman) was passing through the eye of the IRS needle.

EMPLOYMENT AND OPPORTUNITY

At the opposite end of the spectrum are the cruelties of unemployment. Many of these can be avoided by the enactment of an employment tax credit. Under this plan, every time a recession occurred, each employer, large and small, would receive a tax credit of, say, $200 a month for every new employee hired. Such a credit would actually save the government money, for those employed as a result of it would pay income taxes rather than collect unemployment benefits or welfare. It could be lowered and eventually abolished as business conditions improved.

One of the criticisms most frequently made of this proposal is that it would favor expanding companies at the expense of static ones: "Somebody might get a tax credit who was going to hire new workers anyway." This is in fact an argument *for* the tax credit. The only good argument for recessions is that they promote change, by forcing stagnant industries to shrink through bankruptcies and plant closings, thus releasing capital and labor to flow into new areas. A tax measure that pushes along this process would make the changes smoother and the recessions shorter.

There remains the "structural" unemployment problem as it applies in particular to young people and minorities. Here a tax credit for apprenticeship programs in private industry should be a permanent feature of legislation. The alternative is a gilded ghetto of government make-work programs, which offer little permanence, no advancement, and no hope. Voters with a compassion for the disadvantaged must ask themselves whether lasting social and economic improvement will best result from ready entry into the competitive mainstream of society or from government coddling in the backwaters of welfare or guaranteed ghetto jobs.

This leads to even broader questions, alluded to in the beginning of this book. What constitutes fairness in an intrinsically unfair world? What are the mainsprings of human happiness, the pursuit of which is guaranteed in the Constitution? The answers, if one looks around, seem to be grouped under the respective rubrics of security versus hope, equality versus opportunity, protection versus freedom. Most of us would like to have as much as possible of both. We would like to be free to advance, but protected if we fall behind.

Former Secretary of the Treasury William E. Simon puts the dichotomy very cogently—from a conservative point of view:

> Political freedom means only one thing: freedom *from* the state. Franklin Delano Roosevelt, however, invented a new kind of "freedom": a government guarantee of economic security and prosperity. He thus equated 'freedom' with cash. ... By this single ideological switch, FDR caused a flat reversal of the relationship between the individual and the state in America. The state ceased to be viewed as man's most dangerous enemy ... it became man's tenderhearted protector and provider.[2]

Conservatives would do well to recognize, however, that what FDR has done cannot be undone. People will continue to expect protection and prosperity, and they will look to government to provide it, directly or indirectly. To respond to the aspirations of the American people, government must offer the greatest possible measure of both security and freedom. This means keeping the mainstream unclogged, allowing individuals to advance as fast, as far and through as many channels as they can, yet providing a reasonably soft landing for those who fall behind.

This may sound too Darwinian for those neoconservatives of the new left who believe that growth is dead, and that everyone should return to wood stoves without, of course, depleting the forests. But there is no free lunch, even a vegetarian one, in that route. There is also no free lunch to be had from taxing away the opportunities of those who are trying to advance, for it is their efforts that will move society ahead. Finally, there is no free lunch available from the savings of individuals or corporations, for without these savings the economy will consume itself.

It may not be free, but there is a pretty good lunch to be had through encouraging the ambitions, talents, and imaginations of all members of society, allowing scope for progress in new, uncharted directions. The future will be messy, as the past has been. Wrong directions will be chosen, people will be killed or maimed, and the environment sometimes damaged, until inevitable faults are corrected. But, there is no progress without risk. A bunker mentality begets burial.

Capitalism, as Churchill said of Democracy, "is the worst possible system, except for all the others."

EPILOGUE: AN UPDATE

After this manuscript went to the printer, there occurred a new and greater explosion of "money terror." In March, interest rates shot up to 20%, reflecting an inflation rate of almost the same magnitude. This explosion came on the heels of dramatic moves by American monetary authorities to regain control over the runaway expansion of money and credit. The first of these moves occurred October 6, 1979 and was followed by another on March 14, 1980. Predictably, nearly all observers laid the blame for the unprecedented interest rate levels on the six months of attempted restraint by the Federal Reserve Board rather than on a decade of its monetary profligacy.

There are signs, however, that the six months of restraint are beginning to pay off. The fever in commodity markets, particularly gold and silver, has been broken. Interest rates appear to be heading down. Whether the worst is behind us depends upon the determination and ability of the Federal Reserve Board to maintain firm control over money expansion. If the Fed is perceived to be backing off, in the face of Presidential or Congressional pressure, then interest rates will again explode upwards in a new frenzy of money terror.

The great majority of economists are predicting a more severe recession than it predicted a year ago. The milder recession predicted for 1979 did not materialize, but, perhaps, the more severe one destined for 1980 might come to pass. It might, but it need not. Certainly, adjustments, even painful ones, are in prospect. Through a solid decade the nation has been emphasizing consumption—living off its seed grain—at the expense of investment in future growth. This "consumer boom" is coming to an end, but the consumer boom, with the adoption of appropriate tax policies, could be replaced by an investment boom as the source of economic stimulus. This would involve a shift of employment from production for the consumer—automobiles and housing—to production for *future* production—plants and machinery. Such a shift, however painful, does not imply a prolonged recession. But it is vitally necessary to ensure a prolonged recovery.

For an investment boom to take place, tax rates, which are now choking off savings and investment, must be changed. Unfortunately, Congress and the current Administration have moved resolutely in the wrong direction. The recently enacted "windfall profits tax" on oil production (a first in nomenclature that anticipates George Orwell's futurism by four years) serves to raise total income taxes on manufacturing corporations in America by at least thirty percent. Recently, total federal taxes on nonfinancial corporations have averaged some $70 billion per annum. The Orwellian windfall profits tax on oil companies is supposed to raise $240 billion over ten years ($24 billion a year). Unfortunately this tax is levied on the oil produced, rather than on the profits or losses the oil companies may experience. This tax, as with all other corporate taxes, will be paid primarily by consumers, adding, as it does, to the cost of production of each barrel of American oil. At the same time, it will take some $24 billion away from potential private investment in energy each year. This is a rather large bite into the dwindling carcass of our nation's investment potential.

Meanwhile, both President Carter and his Republican opponents have zeroed in on "fiscal discipline" as the paramount issue of the day. Such an approach assumes that one, two, or even ten billion dollars of budget deficit or surplus has any importance in a multitrillion dollar economy in which hundreds of billions of dollars are needed *and can be found* for investment in American industry. The tragedy of this political myopia is that it blocks tax reforms that could create and attract the savings needed for an economic revival.

Reborn fiscal puritans in both parties seem to have chosen the goal of a balanced budget to the exclusion of tax incentives that are desperately needed. Pennywise, they are dollar-Hooverish.

April 15, 1980   William C. Cates

REFERENCES

CHAPTER 1

1. Yemelyanov, A., "The Agrarian Policy of the Party and Structural Advances in Agriculture," *Problemii Ekonomiki,* pp. 22–34, March 1975.
2. *Joint Economic Report,* Senate Report No. 96-44, U.S. Government Printing Office, Washington D.C., p. 26, 1979.
3. Samuelson, Paul A., *Economics,* 10th ed., New York: McGraw-Hill, p. 44, 1976.
4. Op. cit., p. 77.
5. Smith, Adam, *The Money Game,* New York: Random House, 1967.

CHAPTER 2

1. Brown, Lester R., *By Bread Alone,* Praeger, p. 8, 1974.
2. Op. cit., p. 4.
3. Brown, Lester R., *The Global Economic Prospect: New Sources of Economic Stress,* Worldwatch Institute, p. 7, 1978.
4. Allvine, Fred C. and Tarpley, Fred A., Jr, *The New State of the Economy,* Winthrop Publishers, Inc., Chapter 4.
5. Op. cit., p. 9.
6. Denison, Edward F., *Accounting for United States Economic Growth 1929–69,* Brookings Institution, 1974.
7. *Joint Economic Report,* Senate Report No. 96-44, U.S. Government Printing Office, Washington, D.C., p. 26, 1979.

CHAPTER 3

1. Kristol, Irving, *Wall Street Journal,* August 22, 1979.
2. Drucker, Peter F., *Wall Street Journal,* November 3, 1978.
3. Hall, Robert E., *The Nature and Measurement of Unemployment,* National Bureau of Economic Research Working Paper No. 252. July 1978.
4. Clarkson, Kenneth W. and Meiners, Roger E., *Are Unemployment Figures Meaningless?* Business Horizons, Indiana University Graduate School of Business, Vol. 22, February 1979.
5. Galbraith, John Kenneth, *Money,* Houghton Mifflin Company, p. 5, 1975.

CHAPTER 4

1. Keynes, John Maynard, *Economic Consequences of the Peace.* Copyright 1920 by Harcourt Brace Jovanovich, Inc.; renewed 1948 by Lydia Lopokova Keynes. Reprinted by permission of the publisher.
2. Hicks, Sir John, *The Crisis in Keynesian Economics,* Basic Books, p. 2, 1974.
3. Letter to the *New York Times,* December 31, 1933.

CHAPTER 5

1. Friedman, Milton, *Optimum Quantity of Money and Other Essays,* Chicago: Aldine, p. 4, 1969.
2. *Wall Street Journal,* August 24, 1979.

Additional Reading

Anderson, Paul A., "Rational Expectations: How Important for Econometric Policy Analysis," *Quarterly Review,* Federal Reserve Bank of Minneapolis, Fall 1978.
Fama, E. F., "Short-term Interest Rates as Predictors of Inflation," *American Economic Review,* Vol 65, No. 3, 1975.
Fisher, Stanley. "Long-term Contracts, Rational Expectations and the Optimal Money Supply Rule," *Journal of Political Economy,* pp. 191–205, February 1977.
Lucas, R. E. Jr., "Expectations and the Neutrality of Money," *Journal of Economic Theory,* Vol 4, No. 2, 1972.
Sargent, Thomas J. and Wallace, Neil, "Rational Expectations, the Optimal Monetary Instrument and the Optimal Money Supply Rule," *Journal of Political Economy,* Vol. 83, No. 2, 1975.

Brunner, K. and Meltzer, A.H., "Benefits and Costs of Stable Monetary Growth," *Institutional Arrangements and the Inflation Problem.* Vol 3, Carnegie-Rochester Conference Series on Public Policy, New York, North Holland Publishing Company, 1976.

CHAPTER 6

1. Keran, Michael W., "Money and Exchange Rates—1974–1979," *Economic Review,* Federal Reserve Bank of San Francisco, Spring 1979.
2. Wallace, Neil, "Why Markets in Foreign Exchange are Different From Other Markets," *Quarterly Review,* Federal Reserve Bank of Minneapolis, Fall 1979.

Additional Reading

Brittain, Bruce, "Monetary Targets, Interest Rates and Exchange rates," Recherches Economiques de Louvain, Vol 44, No. 3, September 1978.
Dornbusch, R., "Expectations and Exchange Rate Dynamics," *Journal of Political Economy,* Vol 84, No 6, 1976.
Dornbusch, R., "The Theory of Flexible Exchange Rate Regimes and Macroeconomic Policy," *Scandinavian Journal of Economics,* 1977.

CHAPTER 9

1. Editorial, *New York Times,* May 19, 1979.
2. T. Rowe Price Associates, Inc., August 19, 1977.
3. Gilder, George, "Prometheus Bound," Harper's, September 1978.
4. Slemrod, Joel and Feldstein, Martin, "The Lock-in Effect of the Capital Gains Tax: Some Time Series Evidence," National Bureau of Economic Research Working Paper no. 257, July 1978.
5. Galbraith, John Kenneth, *The Great Crash,* Houghton Mifflin Company, p. 30, 1955.

CHAPTER 10

1. Hall, Robert E., *The Nature and Measurement of Unemployment,* National Bureau of Economic Research, Working Paper no. 252, July 1978.
2. Drucker, Peter F., "Meaningful Unemployment Figures," *Wall Street Journal,* November 3, 1978.
3. Cates, William C., "A Tax Kink to Create Jobs," *Wall Street Journal,* December 22, 1975.

4. Joint Economic Committee, *Employment Tax Credits as a Fiscal Policy Tool*, U.S. Government Printing Office, Washington, D.C., 1976.

5. Benjamin, Daniel K. and Kochin, Levis A., "Searching for an Explanation of Unemployment in Interwar Britain," *Journal of Political Economy*, Vol. 87, No. 3, June 1979.

6. Grubel, Herbert, Maki, Dennis, and Sax, Shelley, "Real and Induced Unemployment in Canada," *Canadian Journal of Economics and Political Science*, May 1975.

7. Feldstein, Martin, "The Effects of Unemployment Insurance on Temporary Layoff Unemployment," *American Economic Review*, December 1978.

8. Levitan, Sar A. and Belous, Richard S., *More Than Subsistance, Minimum Wages for the Working Poor*, George Washington University Center for Social Policy Studies.

9. Anderson, Martin, *Welfare, The Political Economy of Welfare Reform in the United States*, Hoover Institution, Stanford University, 1978.

10. Economic Commission for Europe, *L'Emploi des Jeunes*, 1978.

11. Davidson, Lawrence S. and Maddigan, Ruth, *The Conference Overview*, "Business Horizons," Indiana University Graduate School of Business, pp. 43–46, February 1979.

12. Saulnier, Raymond J., Morgan Guaranty Survey, August 1976.

CHAPTER 11

1. Weidenbaum, Murray L., *Business, Government and the Public*, Englewood Cliffs, New Jersey: Prentice Hall, 1977.

2. Weidenbaum, Murray L., The Future of Business Regulation, *AMACOM*, 1979.

3. Clarkson, Kenneth W., Kadlec, Charles W., and Laffer, Arthur B., "Regulating Chrysler Out of Business?," *Regulation Magazine*, September–October 1979.

4. Jacoby, Neil H., Nehemkis, Peter, and Fells, Richard, "Naivete: Foreign Payoffs Law," *California Management Review*, Vol. XXII No. 1, Fall 1979.

5. *New York Times*, June 17, 1979.

6. Smith, Hedrick, *The Russians*, Balentine Books, Chapter 3, 1977.

7. Krauss, Melvin B., "The Social Democracies: Equality Under Strain," *The Wall Street Journal*, February 1, 1980.

CHAPTER 12

1. Editorial, *Wall Street Journal*, October 22, 1979.

2. Simon, William E., "A Time for Truth," Readers Digest Press, p. 113, 1978.

INDEX